WHEN GOD SITS DOWN

RUMINATIONS OF A PRAISER

A 31-DAY DEVOTIONAL

BY TIFFIANY N. COLLIER

FOREWORD BY PASTOR TIMOTHY E. FINDLEY JR.

EDITED BY: CLAUDE R. ROYSTON

ROYSTON
Publishing

BK Royston Publishing
P. O. Box 4321
Jeffersonville, IN 47131
502-802-5385
http://www.bkroystonpublishing.com
bkroystonpublishing@gmail.com

Cover Design: Brent Barnett for besquareddesign.com

ISBN: 978-0-9859439-8-1

Printed in the United States of America

For Evangelist Carolyn Louden
and
In Memory of, Mother Joyce Gilmer,
Who groomed me for Music Ministry

Table of Contents

Foreword   ix

Introduction   xi

Praise is Sexy!   1

Praise Reveals Who God Is   7

Praise for God's Lovingkindness   13

Praise Fits Everybody! (And It's Always   19
in Style...)

Come On, Everybody! Let's Praise the   25
Lord!
Praise in Unity   31

Praise With My Own Voice   37

God Sings Over Me   43

Festival of Praise   49

God Will Complete the Work   55

Bring the Noise. Make it Loud!   61

God Who Sees Who I Am – and Knows   67
My Name

When I'm Overwhelmed – I Will Praise   73

God Gave Me A Song   79

God Is Sovereign – He's a Big God!   85

Celebrating With The Song of My Life   91

The Sacrifice of Praise That Honors God   97

Praise God, My Teacher   103

Praise is My Weapon – Well, At Least One of Them…   109

Wow, God! That's Extraordinary!   115

Give God a "Yet" Praise   121

I Can't Tell It All – But I Can't Wait To Tell It!   127

Praise in the Face of Fear   133

God Thinks About Me! Go Figure!   139

Praise to God, My Security (Better Than ADT!)   145

Choose to Be Thankful   151

Our Hearts Will Sing…   157

God Gives Me A Reason To Laugh   163

Praise God, Who Answers Prayer   169

Praise God With a Childlike Heart   175

**Praise God. Period. (You're Breathing,   181
Ain't You?)**

About the Author   187

FOREWORD

Nearly everyone agrees that praise is good, but very few feel any responsibility to praise God when they don't feel like it. They think that praise is just a response to what happens and that if everything goes right, they will automatically do it. All too often, praise to God is something that many people leave at church, an event that happens only when they come together with other Christians.

However, praise should be a part of a believer's lifestyle, intermingled as a part of their daily prayer life. At work, in the car, at home in bed, or anywhere – praise to the Lord brings the refreshing of the Lord's presence, along with His power and anointing. "I will bless the LORD at all times; His praise shall continually be in my mouth" (Psalms 34:1). Praise is an expression of faith, and a declaration of victory! It declares that we believe God is with us and is in control of the outcome of all our circumstances. Praise is a "sacrifice," something that we offer to God sacrificially, not just because we feel like it, but because we believe in Him and want to please Him!

In this masterfully written devotional, Tiffany Collier thoughtfully and skillfully takes readers on a journey of enlightenment and self-examination!

Her voice and her words, as led by the spirit of God, have been given to the body of Christ. This devotional is one that every person seeking to deepen their roots in Christ should make a part of their daily routine. Enjoy!

Pastor Timothy E. Findley, Jr.

INTRODUCTION

I'm a worship leader. The call to lead people into God's presence is a privilege and an honor. I'm humbled by this opportunity while I am at the same time emboldened and encouraged by it. Before I even realized it, I was being groomed for such a time as this. Having been involved in music ministry for more than 35 years, and having been a worship leader for about 15 of those years, the Lord has presented me with opportunities to go places and to stand before groups of people in order to facilitate a corporate encounter with the Lord. This call is not without its challenges – obedience to God doesn't always produce ideal outcomes. Many times it's just the opposite. I've also been around church a long time, and I've seen a lot of things and met a lot of people who want to do this thing called "leading praise and worship". The church is in dire need of some sort of book that examines modern music ministry – specifically worship leaders, praise teams and the art of leading people into God's presence – and offers some practical instruction on how to properly and more excellently, according to scripture, offer an acceptable, holy offering of praise to the Most High.

This, however, is not that book.

My first exposure to praising the Lord happened when I was a kid. I was sitting in a church service where there was a lot of movement and noise going on. Men and women were screaming, jumping, dancing and falling out. I remember seeing one young woman run up the aisle and out the door. My friend who was a member of that church told me that those people "got the Holy Ghost." I thought he was describing a momentary episode, something that happened to you involuntarily, and then left you when it was over. It was only later when my family joined an Apostolic Pentecostal church that I learned that not only does the Holy Ghost come and live inside of you – it comes to stay! – but that I could also have a relationship with God through Jesus Christ. I also learned that praising God wasn't something that happened to you – it was something you choose to do as an act of your will. Sure, there have been many times when the presence of God moved in a service and I had no choice but to respond to Him. But there have also been many times when I didn't "feel" anything initially; just the memory of His goodness and Who He is to me motivated me to lift my hands and open my mouth to bless His name. There have been many times when life was so hard and I was so broken that giving God glory was the last thing on my mind. In those times I had to command my soul to bless the Lord and make my lips utter praises to the Lord. In giving God glory I've found that He has been the Source of my strength and the Lifter of my head. In those times I found the saying to be true that "the more I praise Him, the better I feel."

For a long time, I've sat in church services where the presence of God was clearly moving and it was evident that His intention was to bless those present, as only He can do. However, I've observed different groups of people in the midst of these services who either are afraid to engage themselves in praise, don't know what to do when His presence shows up, or feel too unworthy to reach out to touch Him. There are also those individuals who have no problem being demonstrative during the corporate worship experience, but lose the sense that the God they serve is accessible outside of the four walls of the sanctuary, and that their singing, dancing, running and other expressions of gratitude and appreciation are only meant for Sundays at 11:00am.

It's great when I'm in the midst of a congregation of like-minded believers, with a praise team and full band to back me up during a worship experience. I feel like David, who also loved being surrounded by the sounds of praise of Israel, and missed terribly when he could not be in the sanctuary of the Lord. However, I've learned that if *I need to get God's attention – if I want to catch His eye –* I don't need to wait on a team of singers, or hear a single instrument, or even be in any church building. All I need to do is think of His goodness, and what He's done for me. I can lift my hands wherever I am at the moment, and I can open my mouth to eulogize, or speak well of, my Lord and my God. I can then offer to Him the sacrifice of thanksgiving and praise from the fruit of my lips. If I'm alone in my house or driving my car, I can raise my voice in a shout to the Lord. If I'm in public, I can just whisper, "Thank You, Jesus," and I know that He sees where I am and, as the older saints used to say, "He comes to see about me just when I need Him most!"

Psalm 22:3 says that the Lord is **enthroned in praise.** Most people say that God "dwells in the midst of praise", but I believe the more accurate understanding is that the praise of the righteous is **where God sits down**. He hears and sees us praising Him and *it gets His attention – it catches His eye!* – **so He comes and sits down**. The King of Kings Himself takes pleasure in my praise; He delights in me! He's the Lord God Almighty, the Source of our strength, and we can find all that we need in Him. When I praise God, He gives me strength. He lifts my head. He binds up and defeats my enemies. He gives me joy and fills me up with His Spirit. The phrase "When praises go up, blessings come down" doesn't appear anywhere in Scripture; the more accurate phrase should be *"When praises go up, God sits down!"* This is when He can render judgments and make decisions on my behalf (Psalm 149).

This devotional is for anyone who wants a more consistent "praise life" – who wants to experience God's presence regardless of present circumstances. The purpose of this devotional is to reinforce the idea to the reader that praise is appropriate at all times. Every day is a day of thanksgiving, because it's a day the Lord has made! We're not going to be in a church building or sanctuary 24/7/365, but God is looking for us to give Him praise that often! We're encouraged to "bless the Lord at all times" – when we're on the mountaintops of triumph, and when we're in the valleys of despair. Psalms records a multitude of emotions shared by each author – even in the worst of times, the writers knew to go to God, for in His presence was everything they needed. Even when they were feeling alone and couldn't hear Him speak, they were confident that He was where they were. If they couldn't trace His hand, they could trust His heart. That's why our God is worthy of praise.

Allow me to bring clarification to the word: **RUMINATION**. This, of course, was one of those words that sounded so precious to my mind, I had to look it up. Believe me, I didn't pick it to show off how much I know; this was another direction of the Holy Spirit. "Rumination" comes from the word "ruminate", which is a synonym for "meditation" or "thinking deeply". The fact is a *ruminant* is a classification of mammal – think cattle, sheep, deer, even giraffes and those kinds of animals, which each have two, three or even four stomachs. These animals can regurgitate food, which has already been chewed and swallowed, from one of their stomachs and "chew the cud". In other words, *rumination* is no more than drawing a thought, idea or memory from the depths of your heart and soul, bringing it to the forefront of your focus, and turning that thought over and over in your mind. Biblical meditation holds a similar connotation, with one muttering a single thought or phrase in order to receive strength, revelation and instruction from it. Feel free to use this devotional in that way.

I am, by no means, an expert on this topic; I, too, am a student. What I share is what the Holy Spirit inspired me to write, whether it's revelation about the scriptures or stories from my own life. Each of the 31 entries is organized in a specific way; each opens with a **title** and a **scripture** from God's Word. The **body of the devotional entry** can speak from several perspectives: reasons and benefits of praise; praising after both success and failure; how God both inspires and inhabits praise; and the kind of praise God looks for and accepts. Each entry is followed by some **questions** that could possibly reframe your praise; you'll have one more motivation to praise, even in the most challenging of situations. There's also **journaling space** following the question for you to write your own answers, stories, testimonies, poetry, songs, etc. — anything that comes to you which enables you to not only praise individually, but will also help you to either share your experiences as well as encourage someone else to share theirs. Some of the passages are going to seem completely random, but my prayer is that every word that's written blesses and impacts you somehow, whether it makes you smile, laugh, cry or just — ruminate. I pray that through God's Word you are provoked to celebrate the God Who is your Source of Everything! I hope you're encouraged by the Word of God to find a reason to praise.

Praise is Sexy!

Rejoice in the Lord, o you righteous! For praise from the upright is beautiful. (Psalm 33:1 NKJV)

Psalm 33 encourages believers to celebrate the Most High with praise. The psalm goes on to tell us how to do it, gives us reasons why we should, and reminds us of God's Sovereignty and power. It tells us why God is worthy of our praise, is the One in Whom we put our trust, and that our ultimate safety and protection is in Him. Verse one says this, in the Amplified Version:

"REJOICE in the Lord, O you [uncompromisingly] righteous [you upright in right standing with God]; for praise is becoming and appropriate for those who are upright [in heart]."

"Rejoice" (Hebrew *ranan,* pronounced raw-NAN*)* means to sing loudly. The writer is saying that appropriate "praise" *(*Hebrew *tehillah,* teh-hil-LAW*)* from the righteous should definitely be audible and visual – it should be a loud and demonstrative celebration of God's marvelous works. Simply put, this kind of praise looks good on the believer.

I think praise is sexy.

I know, I know. That I used the word "sexy" to describe praise like that may be controversial, even offensive to some readers. Let me explain. I'm not talking about praise being sensual in any context. I looked up the word. While the primary definition has to do with provoking carnal interest, other meanings of the word are "appealing", "interesting" or "desirable".

I'm a woman of God, a follower of Christ who truly loves the Lord. I'm not perfect; like most people I make mistakes. But my earnest desire is to pursue God with all that I am, to seek His face more and more, so that I can become more like Him – so that when He looks at me, He will ultimately see a reflection of Himself. My ultimate goal in life is to make God smile.

That being said, I am a woman who is interested in the opposite sex. Occasionally someone will ask me the question about the type of man that interests me. I'm unable to give a proper description as to a specific type. The men I've dated have been black and white; "high-yella" and chocolate; white-collar, blue-collar and no-collar. They've been older and younger; thick and slender; tall and...well, tall-ish – my height or taller. They all had various levels of education, varying interests, diverse careers. I can say they were all believers in Christ, though the denominations varied, as well.

The only common trait I can identify in the men I've been attracted to was this: they were all unashamed praisers and worshippers of God. I don't mean the guys who just show up for church every week and serve in a position, hold an offering plate or occasionally say "Amen" while the preacher delivers his sermon. I'm talking about the ones who don't mind lifting their hands, raising their voices and demonstrating their appreciation for what God has done for them. These men will dance, run, bow, kneel and cry while they praise. Their actions and noises may get other people's attention, but I believe they want their praise to get God's attention above all. I think sincere worship and praise coming from a true man of God unashamed of that kind of public display is super attractive.

I've dated these guys, so I know that none of them were perfect. But for me, there's something about a man who praises God. A brother can look like Jabba the Hutt, but sincere praise can transform him into Idris Elba or Terrence Howard for me.
I'm not the only one who finds praise attractive. God finds it attractive, too. He finds it especially desirable. Authentic praise gets His attention.

It is this loud, public display of celebration that fits the upright especially well. The upright are those whose desire is to please God with not only their behavior, but with their thoughts and intentions. Furthermore, praise from the righteous is appropriate; like a well-tailored suit, or a fabulously-styled outfit, it never goes out of style. Rejoicing is not only acceptable to God, but it's something He expects from us. God loves it when we brag about how strong He is, when we boast to anyone who'll listen about how no one else compares to Him.

He's God — His eyes roam to and fro in the earth, so He sees everybody (Proverbs 15:3). But His gaze is drawn to those who fear Him (Psalm 33:18). It's the praise of the upright that gets — and holds — His attention. John says that God seeks true worshippers, those who will worship Him in spirit and in truth (John 15: 23). God's desire is stirred when the righteous give Him praise.

We never look better to God than when we praise.

DAILY PRAISE: In what way can you make yourself more attractive to God today?

_____
_____
_____
_____
_____
_____
_____
_____
_____
_____
_____
_____
_____
_____
_____
_____
_____
_____
_____
_____
_____
_____
_____
_____
_____
_____

_____

_____

_____

_____

_____

_____

_____

_____

_____

_____

_____

_____

_____

_____

_____

_____

_____

_____

_____

_____

_____

_____

_____

Praise Reveals Who God Is

But ye are a chosen generation, a royal priesthood, an holy nation, a peculiar people; that ye should show forth the praises of him who hath called you out of darkness into his marvelous light: (I Peter 2:9 KJV)

When I was about 12 or 13, I remember looking up the definition of my first name. For some reason, learning what my name meant was important to me. I don't even remember what put this idea into my head, but my curiosity got the best of me. Now this was before personal computers were widely available to everyone, even in places like libraries, so I couldn't research online. There were a lot of books out at the time like "Baby's First Names" for new parents. I eventually found out – don't ask me where – that my name meant "showing a divine appearance of God" or more simply "God revealed".

I was already an unusual child, a very bookish girl with a rather high IQ (tested when I was 5 years old – it made me "Gifted", not "Genius"), a love for all things musical, and a vivid imagination. I would rather read books and watch TV than play with other kids my own age, so I didn't make friends easily. I made up stories and games that I used to entertain myself. But now I had a possible explanation to why I was so different: I was named

7

"God revealed"! That was like saying I was God's Namesake! I was supposed to show God off in a big way! This newfound information let me know that I was special and different and that when people looked at me, they were supposed to see God! This new information excited me, so I was almost bursting to tell someone what I knew. One night the church bus came to pick me up for service (I guess I went to church alone that evening) and I started talking with the bus driver about something. I can't remember how it came up, but I told him that I knew what my name meant. I said, "It means, Showing a divine appearance of God!"

The bus driver burst out laughing.

I went from feeling so special and proud to feeling really embarrassed at my disclosure. His reaction at my statement made me feel some kind of way, like I should have kept my mouth shut. However, sometime later, the man who was driving the church bus that night told me that it wasn't the definition of my name that he found funny; it was the boldness and confidence with which I made that declaration.

Peter's first letter encouraged new believers to understand that they were no longer a part of the world's system, so their behavior and conduct should reflect their new standing in Christ. As they went along in the world, they would be watched; all that they did should represent the Kingdom of God, regardless of what they did for a living or whoever they came in contact with (2:11-18). We are now "living stones", joined together and supported by the "Chief Cornerstone". We are no longer disobedient individuals existing outside of the will of God. Now, we are "a chosen generation" – specifically chosen of God (vs.4). We are "a royal priesthood" – a kingdom of priests (Ex. 19:6, Rev. 1:6) appointed and organized by God himself. We are "a holy nation", sanctified and consecrated for God's special purpose.

God has also called us to be "a peculiar people". The word "peculiar" has a primary definition of something strange or odd – terms that seem to describe me pretty well, from childhood until now. (And having interacted with His people for the last 35+ years, I can say that He has some pretty strange and odd people serving Him. Oh, come on! You know a lot of His people come off as a little weird and…well…different…)

But the secondary definition, the one used here, refers to something belonging exclusively to someone, especially after they've earned it (Greek *peripoiesis,* per-ee-POY-ay-sis). Well, we are God's very own special treasure that was purchased with His own blood. We belong exclusively to Him, and no one else has any rights to us. I BELONG TO GOD! Furthermore, we are supposed to "shew forth the praises of Him who brought us out of darkness into this marvelous light". God never meant for us to be like a fragile possession stashed away in a vault under lock and key — not unlike hiding within church walls. Our lives are to be on full display to the world, because we are the expression of God's glory that needs to be seen by a lost and dying world. That is why we've been called, why our demonstration of His virtues and character have to be carried out.* Regardless of our careers, education, marital status, ethnicity or cultural background, we are Christ's ambassadors called to be His witnesses. Our behavior, our conversation, our gifts, abilities and skills all need to be encountered by the world so that His excellence, His power, His grace and His love can be experienced.

So whether I'm teaching in a classroom, singing in church, paying bills, shopping for groceries or performing onstage, Christ should be revealed in all I do.

*Endicott's Commentary for English Readers

DAILY PRAISE: In what way can you reveal God today? What's the best way you can show Him off in your life as a witness to someone else?

_____

_____

_____

_____

_____

_____

_____

_____

_____

_____

_____

_____

_____

_____

_____

_____

_____

_____

_____

_____

_____

_____

_____

_____

_____

_____

_____

_____

_____

_____

_____

_____

_____

_____

_____

_____

_____

_____

_____

_____

_____

_____

_____

_____

_____

_____

_____

Praise for God's Lovingkindness

Because Your lovingkindness is better than life, My lips shall praise You. (Psalm 63:3 NKJV)

David developed his relationship with God when he was a shepherd in the wilderness, playing his harp, writing poetry and singing songs of worship to the Lord – all while protecting his father's sheep from lions and bears! Such sweet, intimate fellowship David must have had from all that time spent alone with his Creator! (I know that poetry like "The Lord is my Shepherd; I shall not want" wasn't pulled out of thin air simply because David had nothing better to do.)

Fast forward: I can't imagine the kind of discomfort David had to endure in exile from his home country. First, he's minding his own business in the wilderness of Bethlehem, then the next thing he knows, he's summoned before the prophet Samuel to be anointed the next king of Israel. He's then propelled onto the battlefield in the valley of Elah, swinging his sling to take down a giant. Next he's asked to serenade King Saul by playing the lyre (harp) to soothe the monarch's troubled spirit. After this, he's asked to lead King Saul's armies into battle. *In every situation, the favor of God was upon David and the Lord prospered everything that he did.* Up until that point, as far as I can see, that was

13

the only thing that led him into any kind of trouble. I'm sure that he didn't ask to be chased from his home and hunted by King Saul for several years like he was some sort of deadly criminal.

So at the time this Psalm was written, David was a fugitive on the run. He had experienced worship in the Tent of Meeting, more commonly known as the Tabernacle, so he was missing it. But more importantly, he knew personally what it was like to encounter God on a regular basis. However, David as a fugitive was now experiencing God in a new circumstance. The wilderness was probably very similar to that in which he shepherded sheep, with its wild creatures putting his life in peril like with the flocks he protected. Except now, David's peril is magnified by the addition of Saul and his armies.

Let's think of this period in David's life as a backdrop of the best blockbuster/ action/suspense thriller motion picture you've ever seen. David is running for his life, having been set up and betrayed by someone he greatly respected. He's the beloved action hero in this story, with family and close friends (think his wife, Michal, his BFF Jonathan and his go-to guy, Ahimilech the High Priest) to help a brother out in secret. King Saul becomes the super-villain who has an entire army at his disposal, with assassins and scouts out to hunt David down. He's taken a hit out on David and probably has placed a price his head. And David travels to a few places where some very powerful people don't take too kindly to him, and winds up attracting the attention of enemies that he didn't mean to get. So David now has to rope-a-dope his way beneath the nose of his would-be captors, making his way from one town to another, ever staying two steps ahead of the pursuing, angry king. I picture David hiding in caves while he shivers in the cold night air, scurrying up rocky hillsides beneath a hot sun, dodging arrows, ducking spears, starving and dehydrated, afraid to fall asleep at night for fear that Saul would sneak up behind him and —

Wait. I love a good action movie, but I digress...

David more than likely wrote this Psalm while he was in the wilderness of Judaea. In spite of his present situation, in a rough environment with limited resources and very few allies, despite his foes being hot on his heels, David's main thoughts aren't on vengeance on or vindication from his enemies, though he's certain they will get their reward. Neither is his heart set on returning to the comforts of home and convenience of resources at hand, though he has been anointed the new king of Israel. David's primary desire is for _God's presence_; his heart is filled with gratitude at God's steadfast love and his mouth his filled with praises to the Lord! David was so thankful to God for Him keeping him alive, protecting and shielding him from his enemies. But what was more important to David than his own life was God's lovingkindness that He constantly demonstrated; God's grace was the thing David couldn't get enough of. He hungered and thirsted for God's presence more than food and drink. He understood that his own life was temporary and finite, but God's lovingkindness was an eternal, limitless supply.

The word "lovingkindness" is from the same Hebrew word (*chacad*, pronounced khaw-SAD) referred to repeatedly in Lamentations 3:22-23: "It is of the LORD's *mercies* that we are not consumed, because his *compassions* fail not. *They* are new every morning: great is Thy faithfulness." This passage has been one of my favorites for years, because I have found God's lovingkindness toward me to be constant, in spite of trial, adversity and personal failure. So of course, these verses are the basis for one of my favorite hymns, the sentiment of which, I believe, David would have shared:

Great is Thy faithfulness! Great is Thy faithfulness!
Morning by morning, new mercies I see!
All I have needed, Thy hand has provided —
Great is Thy faithfulness, Lord, unto me!
— "Great Is Thy Faithfulness," William M. Runyan and Thomas O. Chisolm, 1923

DAILY PRAISE: List three things that God has done most recently to demonstrate His lovingkindness to you.

_____
_____
_____
_____
_____
_____
_____
_____
_____
_____
_____
_____
_____
_____
_____
_____
_____
_____
_____
_____
_____
_____
_____

_____

_____

_____

_____

_____

_____

_____

_____

_____

_____

_____

_____

_____

_____

_____

_____

_____

_____

_____

_____

_____

_____

Praise Fits Everybody! (And It's Always in Style...)

To appoint unto them that mourn in Zion, to give unto them beauty for ashes, the oil of joy for mourning, <u>the garment of praise for the spirit of heaviness</u>; that they might be called trees of righteousness, the planting of the LORD, that he might be glorified. (Isaiah 61:3 KJV, emphasis mine)

To grant [consolation and joy] to those who mourn in Zion — to give them an ornament (a garland or diadem) of beauty instead of ashes, the oil of joy instead of mourning, <u>the garment [expressive] of praise instead of a heavy, burdened, and failing spirit</u> — that they might be called oaks of righteousness [lofty, strong, and magnificent, distinguished for uprightness, justice and right standing with God], the planting of the Lord, that He might be glorified. (Amplified)

Arthur Samuel Joseph said that singing is probably the most hedonistic activity humans perform. For most people, the primary objective for singing isn't to become famous, to make any money or to win any awards; we sing simply because it feels good (even if it doesn't sound all that great; it pains me when my voice isn't functioning like as I'd like). Since I was a kid, I've always sung or hummed, sometimes unconsciously; it's second nature to me, like breathing. But regardless of the ability of the singer, I believe it's safe to say that, for one's own enjoyment, it's easy to do. And it doesn't matter if one is in a car, a shower, a work cubicle, or walking down the street.

Eventually, and fortunately, I learned about praise and worship, what it does, what it was, and what it wasn't. I learned that praise didn't always mean singing; there were different kinds of ways to praise God. I also discovered that God dwells, or is enthroned, in the praises of his people. Psalm 22:3 uses the word *tehillah*, which means song of praise. Apparently, it's the praise where God sits down.

Let me digress for a moment. Louisville is most famous for the Kentucky Derby — the annual "Run for the Roses" at Churchill Downs, most often referred to as "The Most Exciting 2 Minutes in Sports". So beginning in the month of March, there are a great number of festivities planned in the city of Louisville leading up all the way up until Derby Day — the first Saturday in May. In 2014, at the Kentucky Center for the Arts, I attended the "Grace at the Race" concert featuring Amy Grant, Tamela Mann and Kirk Franklin. People asked me what I was going to wear to the event, with good reason; Derby is a season of the year known for its spring fashion and headgear (hats, fascinators, etc.). Sure enough, that night at the KCA there was a parade of after-six attire, along with spring sundresses and ornate hats and fascinators. Because I didn't attend the banquet which preceded the event, I dressed in what I considered to be stylish comfort in JAG jeans and a Guess tweed and leather jacket. I simply didn't want to worry about the attempt to get to my seat, walking through a packed row, trying not to step on people's feet, and doing all of that in sparkly evening sandals, pulling either on a cocktail dress or an evening gown. And then, possibly, fidgeting in my chair in discomfort during the concert, wishing I'd simply brought a pair of flats and dreading the walk back to the car. (You'd actually have to have been inside this KCA's Whitney Hall to appreciate what I'm saying.) But because I was comfortable in my clothes that night, and not worried about trying to dress to impress, I had none of those concerns. I just sat back and enjoyed the concert.

Make no mistake, I love fashion! But consider something with me; think for a second about the clothes in your closet. All of us probably have items in our wardrobe that may not flatter us all that well, but we purchased it either because we saw it on sale, or we saw it on someone else. There are also things we own that may look good on us, but only after a moderate amount of pulling, tugging and fixing. How many clothes do we have that are easy to put on our bodies, actually look good and are also comfortable to wear?

Isaiah 61:3 says that God performs a great exchange. For the downtrodden, the depressed, the brokenhearted, He offers several things for the purposes of elevation, justification, establishment and strength. One of the items God gives to us is a _garment of praise_ in place of a spirit of heaviness. This "garment" (Hebrew _maateh_, pronounced mah-at-TEH) means a wrap or a mantle. This garment God gives us is something very simple to put on, not a robe or a tunic or a cloak. He gives us something that no matter where we are or what we're doing, we can put it on, in order to create an atmosphere where we can meet Him, and he can lift us and strengthen our spirits for whatever we may be facing.

And guess what? This garment looks good on everybody! For real, though. Don't believe me? Psalm 33:1 says, "Rejoice (_ranan_, raw-NAN: _to shout for joy, give a ringing cry, cry out_) in the Lord, oh ye righteous: for praise (_tehillah_, teh-hil-LAW) is comely (_naveh_, naw-VEH: _seemly, comely, beautiful_) for the upright." Regardless of skin tone, size, shape, gender or ethnicity - this garment makes us more attractive to God. When we're wearing this garment, we look so good to

Him that He sits down and takes pleasure in our praise.

Oh, and the garment of praise He gives to us is a song (*tehillah*). So we don't have to be professional or gifted singers to get God's attention. As long as it's sincere praise to Him, He loves it. It doesn't matter if your voice isn't the greatest sounding to anyone else, or even to yourself. God loves it every time you sing to Him.

The One Who loves us makes it easy for us to experience His presence when we need Him. So put it on!

DAILY PRAISE: What heaviness has the "garment of praise" replaced in your life? Who else can you encourage to put on this "garment"?

_____

_____

_____

_____

_____

_____

_____

_____

_____

_____

_____

_____

_____

_____

_____

_____

_____

_____

_____

_____

_____

_____

_____

Come On, Everybody! Let's Praise the Lord!

Let the word of Christ dwell in you richly, teaching and admonishing one another in all wisdom, singing psalms and hymns and spiritual songs, with thankfulness in your hearts to God. Colossians 3:16 ESV

I grew up in an Apostolic Pentecostal Holiness church. My Christian experience started in a small Baptist church, but the Apostolic church exposed me to most everything I learned about church. Let me begin by saying that I lived for a time in a neighborhood where there was a church on just about every corner, and starting at age 9, I made it my mission to visit just about all of them! So at age 12, when our family got to this holiness church, my mind was blown – everything was brand new to me. I started seeing stuff that I had never seen before! The building was larger, music and the singing was better, the preaching was more interesting, and everyone praised the Lord! I was used to adults and old folks "catching the Holy Ghost", but I had never seen kids my age raise their hands, dance and shout until I got to this place.

One of my favorite things about the church was a part of the program they called "Praise Service". This was the time when people could stand up and talk about the goodness of the Lord. Some people sang songs, other people quoted Bible verses. But most people told stories about what God had done for them. I heard so many people talk about needs that they had, and God provided for them, whether it was God replacing a broken-down vehicle with a new one, or if it was a growing family being blessed to buy a new home. There were young men who spoke of God blessing them with a job, or single moms praising God for healing their sick child. Even kids and teenagers would stand, some with tears rolling down their faces, thanking God for protecting them from a school bully, or walking away from a car accident. There were brand-new, born-again Christians who were so glad to be saved they could barely contain their praise, and old saints who talked about the Lord keeping them "down through the years" and bringing them from "a mighty long way."

I suppose that the best testimonies to me were about the power God so drastically changing someone from the inside out. It was amazing how different these church folk were from the way they said that they used to be. From looking at them, I would never imagine that the members at my church were ex-prostitutes, ex-pimps, ex-drug dealers and ex-drug addicts. They had been alcoholics, cigarette smokers, thieves and cussers. Some of these now men and women of God used to love a good fight — they would just as well cut you as look at you. One man gave a testimony about being accused of wrongdoing by a co-worker. This brother found himself with his accuser in his boss' work trailer on the construction work site. This man was just trying to do a job, not have his job in jeopardy, but he stood silently in front of his supervisor, not defending himself, while listening to his co-worker say negative things about him that simply weren't true. I'll interject here that this brother from the church wasn't a small man, either; at the time I think he stood 6'3" and weighed about 350 pounds or so. The great thing about this incident, he said, was that he realized how much the Lord had changed him, because his "old-self" would have slammed this guy into a wall!

"Old man" versus "new man" is a primary theme of Colossians 3. Before Christ, our nature was filled with sexual immorality, impurity, covetousness, anger, malice, evil desire, corrupt communication and things like that. Since we are now risen with Christ, we either put off those old things or put to them death. Now, as new creatures in Christ, we put on compassionate hearts, meekness, patience, kindness, with forgiveness and forbearance, wrapping everything in love. We have set our minds to be more like Christ as He transforms us, and the Word of God is the standard by which we live. We are supposed to come together and teach and encourage each other about the gospel of Jesus Christ; we're supposed to testify to one another about His goodness. We're supposed to use songs, hymns and spiritual songs to express His wonderful work that He's performing from the inside out. Testimonies, or praise reports, or whatever you may call them — we use these to remind ourselves, and one another, that the old man has died. The new man is risen with Christ. The Word of God never fails. And the Holy Ghost continues to do the transforming work in our lives. Reminds me of a hymn the Senior Choir used to sing:

Since Jesus came into my heart! Since Jesus came into my heart!
Floods of joy o'er my soul, like the sea billows roll,
Since Jesus came into my heart!
— Rufus H. McDaniel, 1914 (Public Domain)

There's been a great change in me! Great change in me!
I am so happy! I am so free
Since Jesus brought me out of darkness into the marvelous light —
Oh, oh, oh, oh! Great change in me!
— Composer Unknown (Public Domain)

I was too young to understand the song then, but I do now, when they sang:

Something on the inside working on the outside —
oh, what a change in my life!

DAILY PRAISE: What great change has God performed in your life? Write down a testimony that illustrates that great change. Who needs to hear your story?

_____

_____

_____

_____

_____

_____

_____

_____

_____

_____

_____

_____

_____

_____

_____

_____

_____

_____

_____

Praise in Unity

May the God of endurance and encouragement grant you to live in such harmony with one another, in accord with Christ Jesus, that together you may with one voice glorify the God and Father of our Lord Jesus Christ. Therefore welcome one another as Christ has welcomed you, for the glory of God. Romans 15:5-7 ESV

The early church had issues — lots of issues that Paul had to address in letters that he wrote to several churches. Sure, there was power and demonstration of the Holy Ghost, miracles, signs and wonders. The Holy Ghost manifested spiritual gifts galore, as well as many ministry gifts among the believers. But the church was, and still is, made up of imperfect human beings. Spirit-filled individuals, yes, who understood that God is love, and that the fruit of the Spirit is love — but who, on occasion, and unintentionally, got on one another's nerves.

Not much has changed, has it?

Why else would Paul talk extensively (Romans 14) about believers eating meats that were sacrificed to idols? I mean, surely Spirit-filled believers know that meat is just meat, and false idols have no power anyway, so it shouldn't matter if I'm eating it, right? Paul explains individuals who are "strong", or have that knowledge, shouldn't throw their knowledge in the face of the "weak", or those who may be ignorant of that information. If someone learned it was wrong to eat it, then seeing another believer eating that meat may cause them a problem. Paul said while we may have the freedom to eat the meat, our love for the "weaker" Christian needs to motivate us to not eat it, so we don't cause our brother to stumble. Paul goes on in chapter 15 to tell us that those of us who are strong ought to bear the infirmities of the weak. In other words, our liberties shouldn't serve our selfishness, but we should go out of our way to please, or put up with, the spiritual needs of our brother, in order to build them up.

I have personally struggled with indulging the comfort of pleasing myself versus the inconvenience of accommodating my neighbor. It still remains a challenge on some level, even all these many years later. But I used to really bother God with my queries:

If the brothers are having a problem with what the sisters are wearing, why can't they just avoid looking? Why do I have to fix what I'm wearing? Aren't they saved? Perhaps they just need to take a cold shower...

What is the big deal about wearing slacks to their church? Don't they know that Deuteronomy 22:5 has nothing to do with women wearing pants? I'm still saved. I'm still anointed. I should be able to go and worship regardless of what I'm wearing...

Here's an example closer to home: when I was kid, my mother started bringing home a lot of "strays". I'm not talking about four-legged animals, either. I mean, she would bring these strange people into our home that I under normal circumstances would have nothing to do with (of course, I had no control over who she welcomed to our home). I think just about all of these people were new to the church. It may have been that other church folk didn't have that much to do with these new members. Some of them looked funny; some of them smelled funny, too. Some were mentally or emotionally challenged. Sometimes, it wasn't that they were so different; some of them had no place to go, so she invited them to stay and live with us for a while. As a teenager I'm thinking, *What? Are you kidding? We don't have that much to begin with; now we have to share it with them?*

The thing about mom was that she had this compassionate heart. She hated to see people down and wanted to do all she could to lift them up. She gave to new Christians unconditionally, whether it was a meal or a bed. Sometimes she just spent time with someone – either in person for an afternoon out or a long phone conversation, listening to them vent about the tough times they were going through. Perhaps she was so kind to them because she knew all too well what it felt like not to have, and she remembered when others helped her out. Even today, all these many years later, she's always trying to take care of someone less fortunate. She's patient with these "strays" because she knew someone had been patient with her once. She exemplified the teaching of the Apostle Paul, inconveniencing herself to serve someone else. This is the mindset that all believers need to have one toward another: building one another up with patient service and encouragement. Christ is the one Who encourages us, is patient with us, and welcomes us – and we ought to come together with one mind and one voice, all for the glory of God. This is the way that God is truly glorified, as we become more like Him.

I suppose that's why I don't really believe in tolerance, as most people see it. Tolerating people doesn't require anything of me other than my acknowledgement that they exist. Love, on the other hand, requires giving. Can you imagine tolerance replacing love in John 3:16? *"For God so **tolerated** the world... "* He would have never sent Jesus to die on the cross; we'd all still be lost in sin. Love requires demonstration so that the world will see it: "By this shall all men know that ye are my disciples, if ye have love one to another." (John 13:35)

My mom was a good teacher to both myself and my sister. I think my sister has my mom's compassionate heart, having opened her home on one occasion or another first to her own friends, then to her children's friends. She'll feed or give the shirt off of her back to someone if she thinks they need it. I've learned that I need to extend a hand to anyone who's in need, regardless of how different they are from me. The love of God in my life requires me to exit my comfort zone. Let's come together as the church, in love and service, so that everyone will see our good deeds and praise our Heavenly Father (Matthew 5:16).

DAILY PRAISE: Think about your local church or congregation. Which people do you find challenging to deal with? How can you better accommodate others in your life so that God is glorified?

_____

_____

_____

_____

_____

_____

_____

_____

_____

_____

_____

_____

_____

_____

_____

_____

_____

_____

Praise With My Own Voice

I will sing to the Lord as long as I live; I will sing praise to my God while I have being. Psalm 104:33 ESV

I remember hearing that scripture for the first time in a song written and sung by Kristle Murden on her album "I Can't Let Go" (1980). I remember listening to the radio and hearing her distinctive voice singing with Andrae Crouch on one of his early projects. Her soprano voice was so clear and pretty, and I remember thinking, "Man, I wish I could sing like that."

I believe that was a recurring thought in my head when I was a kid. I started singing when I was a kid, yeah, and I thought my voice was okay. Those were the times when I was by myself, singing in our bathroom, or walking to the bus stop. I would unconsciously hum under my breath and wouldn't necessarily be aware of it until someone else would comment on it, either with a compliment or a plea for me to stop. It was only when I started listening more to the radio or to records that I became acutely aware of what my voice was lacking compared to the others that I heard. I envied so many remarkable voices that I heard or saw: the soaring, sustaining notes sung by Barbara Streisand and Tramaine Hawkins; the colorful runs and trills performed by Teena Marie or any one of the Clark Sisters; the forceful belts of Patti Labelle, Chaka Khan or Shirley Ceasar. I listened to the achingly sweet tones of Olivia Newton-John and Twila Paris and the vocal stylings of Nancy Wilson and Dottie Jones (of the Richard Smallwood Singers). As much as I longed to mimic or duplicate what they did, I came up remarkably short. I couldn't make my voice do what they did.

I didn't have to only listen to the radio or watch TV to hear great singing. I could just show up at church on Sunday morning and hear many a sister lay it out just as powerfully and beautifully. I could travel to a State Council meeting or a National Convention and hear many voices that were yet unknown and unsigned to any record label. I recall attending my first national conference in Cincinnati, Ohio in 1980 and sitting in a service being blown away by one particular voice that led this amazing choir. I heard this woman solo on a song made popular by the Clark Sisters at the time – the choir that night tore that song up! – and I was simply in awe of her gift, wishing I could have a voice like that. I never saw or heard her at another convention, but it was almost 30 years later when I discovered who that singer was, and realized that I had listened to her for years on the radio. The singer's name was Shirley Murdock, and her song "As We Lay" became a hit single only a few years after I heard her sing during that church service.

In the meantime, I sang in my church's choirs, first the youth choir, then a series of groups, then, when I got older, with adult choirs. I served first as a member, then as a soloist, then as a choir director, conducting rehearsals and teaching parts. For many years, I was a wannabe soprano – I had an alto range but I was in denial, wanting to sing what I thought were the good parts and high melodies that the soprano section frequently sang. Because of the mistreatment I gave my voice I was occasionally hoarse; eventually, somewhere in my 20s, I lost the top third of my vocal range. This happened during a time when I was directing and teaching 3 church choirs, singing with a group which was increasingly in demand for engagements, and performing in and touring with a gospel musical stage production. I struggled with that loss for almost a year. I eventually recovered, but I knew I had to make changes in the way I used my voice.

It was then I began to appreciate what I had, and to learn what my own voice could and couldn't do. I started to realize that while I sang other people's music, my praise was my own, and my voice was a part of my praise. Perhaps I couldn't riff and run like Dorinda Clark-Cole or sing high notes like Sandy Patti, but God didn't expect me to sing like them, because He didn't give me what they had. He gave me my own voice with which to offer my own authentic praise. And about the time I came to terms with what God had given me vocally, I was given the opportunity to lead other people into His presence, through song. One of the great voices I admired so in my youth began to mentor me in leading worship. So now I sing and lead other people into His Presence as a worship leader. Now I'm able to share my experiences of God's power in my life, using my own authentic sound, making other people's songs my own, sharing them in my own way.

I have my own testimony with which I can use my voice to share what God has done for me. The church elders used to sing, "You can't tell it, let me tell it, what He's done for me! You don't know like I know what He's done for me! I get joy when I think about what He's done for me!"

So I sing. I use the voice to tell the story of what God has done for me. I sing about my failures, my down times, my struggles. I also sing about His majesty, His faithfulness, His power, the victories He's won. I'll sing in a sanctuary. I'll sing in the park. I'll sing to thousands, or hundreds, or just a few. I still sing in the bathroom, and I still sing on my way to the bus stop. I'll continue sing His praise to Him as long as the Lord allows me to have breath, and a memory, and a voice of my own.

DAILY PRAISE: Maybe you have the gift to sing, or perhaps you don't think you can sing that well. In any case, what song can you use your voice to sing to the Lord today?

_____

_____

_____

_____

_____

_____

_____

_____

_____

_____

_____

_____

_____

_____

_____

_____

_____

_____

_____

_____

God Sings Over Me

The LORD your God is in your midst, a mighty one who will save; he will rejoice over you with gladness; he will quiet you by his love; he will exult over you with loud singing. Zephaniah 3:17 ESV

The group Commissioned sang a song back in the 80s titled "When Jesus Sings". It was composed by Fred Hammond. Here are some of the lyrics:

"A gift truly given to man is a voice to sing/And some do so well/A voice of gold and silk it seems they have…"

There is so much new talent in the music industry today, and so much fanfare over the most current sound of style of singing, that I truly believe that each generation thinks that they invented singing. With every raspy tone, or fancy trill or run, of rhythmic progression of words, we impress ourselves more and more, as if to say, "Look what I/we can do!" With shows like *American Idol, The Voice*, and *The X-Factor*, it's no wonder that we all don't want to be "discovered" and acquire instant fame and celebrity. And these days, you only have to be in the right place at the right time, whether that's in a subway in New York, on a street corner in Mississippi, or on a YouTube channel to be discovered (just ask Justin Beiber about that last piece).

Even the gospel music industry has jumped on board, and, in the name of giving "psalmists" a "platform", have created Sunday Best, so that we can "ooh" and "aah" even further at the great "anointing" and "presence of God" demonstrated through soaring ranges and loud squalling, all while performing what could turn out to be the next major Praise and Worship ballad or anthem.

Please. Give me a break.

"It seems today some sing about almost anything/And there is no life/There's just a rhythm and a rhyme..."

I've been a part of music ministry for the majority of my life, and I've witnessed the music industry as a whole morph from 8-tracks to digital downloads. But that's just media. Recordings have moved from a pretty raw, live sound to slick mixing, overdubbing and auto-tuning. And let's not talk about the fact that a lot of these so-called performers and entertainers don't even sing live — it's all lip syncing — so we might have to call their "talent" into question. (Can anybody say "Milli Vanilli"?) In addition to that, there's a lot of popular music circulating that has little impact on the masses beyond a looped track of beats which provoke dancing and movement. These days, you can place a line of lyrics containing little more than the right syncopation on top of the instrumentation, and bam – you have a chart-topping Billboard hit.

Don't get me wrong. I call myself a "musical mutt". I love music. All kinds of music. I believe it's safe to say that, as far as any genre is concerned, if it's music, I like it. My question is, What happened to the substance? Where's the meaning? Has everything been reduced to clichés and catchphrases? I can even ask this about some gospel and Christian music nowadays. I just really appreciate music that has a real message – something that pierces the heart, that either makes me shout, cry or really think. Not too many artists and composers' music affects me in that way.

"The day He sang, it was so pure/A sound so clear that I've never heard before/A song of refreshing to the soul of man/Lord here I am, please sing again…"

Zephaniah's prophecy begins with gloom and doom, spelling out God's judgment against the nation of Israel for their pride, their disobedience, for their selfishness and self-centeredness. Zephaniah especially notes the sins of the priests and prophets – the leadership who held positions of influence who were supposed to turn the people's focus to God, not away from Him. For these reasons God would allow disaster to fall upon His chosen people. But because God still loved them, there would come a day, says the prophet, when a remnant of Israel would be restored back to Jerusalem – those who would see their need for the LORD God and call upon Him, those who would recognize their sin and ask for His forgiveness, those would humbly return to Him ready to serve. Then God would pour out judgment on the nations who were enemies to Israel, those who antagonized and drove His people into exile. He promised that they would have no reason to fear any longer and He encourages them to sing and praise the Lord. The Lord would be with them - the humble, trusting, obedient remnant – and the Lord would be so in love with His chosen, He would burst into song. God would sing over them who pleased Him – sing over them whom He loved so much.

"To escape from the cares of this life, I need to hear You sing over and over/A song of Your Word that puts life in men to help them stand for You much bolder…"

Song, and singing, is God's idea. He's made it easy for humans to do it, but I find it amazing that He does it Himself. GOD SINGS! AND HE DOES IT FOR ME! When I please Him, when I trust Him, when I obey Him, when I serve Him, He sings over me. He has written a song for my life that He is singing.

My desire, ultimately, is to join in singing the song with Him. I want my life to join in singing the song in a duet with the Almighty.

DAILY PRAISE: Take a moment and listen to the Holy Spirit as He speaks to you. What song can you hear God singing over you?

_____

_____

_____

_____

_____

_____

_____

_____

_____

_____

_____

_____

_____

_____

_____

_____

_____

_____

_____

_____

_____

Festival of Praise

Many sacrifices were offered on that joyous day, for God had given the people cause for great joy. The women and children also participated in the celebration, and the joy of the people of Jerusalem could be heard far away. Nehemiah 12:43 (NLT)

"This is a CELEBRATE!" Leroy Brown aka Mr. Brown, Tyler Perry's Meet the Browns

I love a celebration. I get a thrill when I'm able to attend a party of just about any kind. Most parties that I know of mark an occasion of some sort – a birthday, a wedding, a graduation, a going-away event, a housewarming, a bridal or baby shower, etc. I look forward to the goings-on, whether it's running into old friends or making new acquaintances. I love moving to the music, either alone, with a partner or in a line dance; it doesn't matter if the music is provided from a stereo, a DJ, a live band or someone's playlist on their phone. Games are always fun, whether it's cards (Spades, anyone?), Scrabble (my personal favorite), or a volleyball match in the yard outside (though my aim sucks!). And of course, at any party, you have to have good food: finger sandwiches, chicken wings, Swedish meatballs, hot dogs and burgers and good barbecued anything! (Just be sure to provide a relish tray – I've got to have my veggies!)

I digress. The best parties are held to commemorate a specific milestone in the life of a person, family or community. The triumph of a high school or college graduate is not only that of the student, though they alone receive the specific recognition. It also belongs to the parents, family or loved ones who provided support for that student. Same goes to the individuals who join in holy matrimony, for the families share in the joy of two lives becoming one, and they celebrate the future that this new couple's story will write. The reason to rejoice is not just in that moment, but because of all that these individuals went through to get to that moment. The studying, the planning, the preparation – it doesn't matter the amount of time spent to reach the goal, whether in days, months or years. The sense of accomplishment one has is a wonderful thing, but it can be made all the more sweet sharing that with people who were there for us, and that is what matters. Sure, I can praise God by myself for what He's done, and for what He's brought me through. But there's nothing like corporate praise. I mean, being with like-minded believers, knowing that what we've come through, or what He's enabled us to accomplish – the jubilation that occurs when a group of people are in one accord with praising God!

So with everything Nehemiah endured, he had a reason to rejoice — God answered his prayer. He expressed his heart's desire to the Lord, and the Lord fulfilled the desire of his heart. Nehemiah learned that the wall around Jerusalem was in ruins, therefore making the city unsafe for its current inhabitants and vulnerable to any enemies wanting to take advantage. Nehemiah prayed one prayer, and God soon after granted his request. Nehemiah was King Artaxerxes' cupbearer (that name is a mouthful!), and when the king saw Nehemiah's distress, he asked him what the problem was. When Nehemiah requested time and resources to rebuild the wall, the king gave him all that he asked for. When Nehemiah posed the challenge to the leaders, city officials and priests, they immediate agreed to rebuild the wall. They strategized to have groups of men work on each of the gates of the wall surrounding the city, and these men worked, day and night. Enemies came to discourage and distract Nehemiah from completing the work; he prayed again to the Lord, and encouraged the people. While the people continued to build, the Lord thwarted the plans of their enemies. And the wall, which took years to build initially, was completed and repaired in 52 days.

This was a reason to celebrate! A group of the priests, Levites and singers came back to the city, ready to serve in their posts. The Feast of Tabernacles was reinstituted and the Book of the Law was read to the people each of the seven days of the Feast. The people began to weep when they heard the Word of God, but Nehemiah encouraged them to eat, drink and share with those who didn't have anything. This feast was holy unto the Lord, and the people didn't need to worry, because the joy of the Lord was their strength (Nehemiah 8:10).

Soon after, there was a wall dedication ceremony filled with splendor, pomp and pageantry! There was an orchestra filled with harps, lyres and cymbals; the priests blew the trumpets. And there were two choirs which sang to one another of the wonderful works of God! The musicians played, the singers sang, and everyone – men, women and children – took part in the celebration, so much so that, based on what the scripture says, cities all around Jerusalem could hear the sounds of celebration. And the people rejoiced...because God had given them great joy!

Now, that's a party.

What has God done for you and your people that's worth a celebration? Go ahead – share what God has done with the congregation of believers. I bet we'll all join in the praise with you. The Lord is worthy of the praise! "Oh magnify the Lord with me; and let us exalt His Name together!" (Psalm 34:3)

Hey, what can I say? I love a good party!

DAILY PRAISE: What has God done for you and your family that's worth a celebration? What was the last public praise report you shared?

_____
_____
_____
_____
_____
_____
_____
_____
_____
_____
_____
_____
_____
_____
_____
_____
_____
_____
_____
_____

God Will Complete the Work

And David said to Solomon his son, "Be strong and courageous and do it. Do not be afraid and do not be dismayed, for the LORD God, even my God, is with you. He will not leave you or forsake you, until all the work for the service of the house of the LORD is finished." I Chronicles 28:20 (ESV)

Just do it. Nike

How overwhelmed must Solomon have felt at the thought of completing such a monumental task of building the Temple? This was the vision that his father David had, to build a house for God to dwell in: he had collected and contributed all of the materials needed for the construction – precious metals and stone, down to the last nail - and hired the builders and the craftsmen. He'd assembled and given instructions to the priests, the Levites and the leaders of the Israel. Then he had given this assignment to his son, Solomon, for him to complete, and in doing this he would fulfill his father's heart's desire. He knew that his son was young and inexperienced, but he encouraged Solomon in this way: "Be strong and courageous! Take action – move forward! Don't be afraid! Don't be discouraged! Don't panic! I know that the God that I serve – the One Who has shown Himself faithful to me all of these years – will be with you

55

throughout this entire process. He won't abandon you; He won't walk off and leave you, and He won't fail you. He'll guide you and see to it that everything having to do with building, outfitting, furnishing and staffing the Temple of the LORD is correctly and completely finished. Everything and everyone you need to do the job has been provided for you. Just say the word. Get up. Get started. Get moving. Just do it!"

Wow. I have a problem just balancing my checkbook on a regular basis.

I won't even tell you about the challenges just in writing this book...

Writing this particular entry got me looking back at some challenging projects in my own life. I was the first in my immediate family to go to college, so that idea alone was overwhelming. I was facing the prospect of going to college and all that came along with it: applications for admissions, tests, scholarships and financial aid. I didn't think about it then, but each year would roll around and I'd complete more application forms for one thing or another, get word that the financial aid/scholarship money had paid the tuition and fees, go register for classes, get my schedule, purchase textbooks, start attending classes, begin studying and completing assignments, so on and so forth. Fulfilling the requirements for a degree seemed insurmountable, though many had done it before, but looking at it from the starting point, I can honestly say that it wasn't a sure thing that I would reach the goal; frankly, I couldn't see that far. Thankfully, I had a supportive mother and an entire church family encouraging and praying for me. The academic scholarship took care of the tuition and fees; the federal and state loans and grants took care of most of the rest of the expenses. It was hard work, no doubt, and while I was doing it, it felt like it was taking forever. But finally, one day in the winter of 1989, I pulled the etched parchment out of a cardboard tube that said that I had indeed fulfilled the coursework requirements that entitled me a Bachelor of Arts degree. And in the spring of 1990, I looked back at those 5½ years of academic achievement, and walked across a stage along with hundreds of other people commemorating the attainment of a years-long goal.

My mind wanders back even further in time, and I remember that when I was a child, I used to sit in church during testimony services and listen to people talk about how long they had been saved. They'd recount the kind of person that they used to be and marvel at the person they'd become in

Christ. A common statement made was, "I'm not where I want to be, but I praise God that I'm not who I used to be." And then they'd thank God for His keeping power – the Lord had kept them saved for 5, 10, 20 years. The older saints – the "mothers" of the church, the respected older "fathers", those with the "hoary heads" which indicated wisdom – would stand up – some with walkers, some with canes, and some who they'd just give a microphone to while they sat – and thank God for being saved for forty years. Fifty years. A few could testify that they came to know Christ as a child. I'd just sit in amazement as a new "babe in Christ", just a kid, barely a teenager, and think to myself, "Wow. They've been saved that long? Is that really possible?" Trying to imagine that length of time was just, well, overwhelming for me.

Now, I give God praise for a memory – and the ability to finish what I started. I look back at all that God has helped me to endure and allowed me to accomplish. I can certainly say, without a shadow of doubt, God was there with me, guiding, teaching and directing me. He never left me. He never failed me. He made sure I had all that I needed, in resources and in people. He's surrounded me with His Body – a family of believers who have, down through the years, prayed for me, corrected me, encouraged me, supported me. He gave me salvation. He filled me with His Spirit. According to I Corinthians 6:19, He's made me His temple. And boy, do I need work! And He's given me His Word, His promises which say, "…He who has begun a good work in you will [continue to] perfect and complete it until the day of Christ Jesus [the time of His return]." (Phil. 1:6, Amplified)

DAILY PRAISE: What task are you attempting to finish in your life right now? What work is God completing in you?

_____

_____

_____

_____

_____

_____

_____

_____

_____

_____

_____

_____

_____

_____

_____

_____

_____

_____

_____

_____

Bring the Noise. Make it Loud!

"Make a joyful noise unto the Lord, all ye lands. Serve the Lord with gladness: come before His presence with singing." Psalm 100:1, 2 (KJV)

These verses could be paraphrased to simply say, "Praise God LOUDLY. Serve Him GLADLY. And when you come into His presence, SING LOUDLY."

At the time of writing this, I've just jumped off of a friend's Periscope "Pass the Mic" challenge. He takes a night, starts a live broadcast, invites his friends – a lot of whom are accomplished musicians and singers – and we take turns broadcasting while singing from whatever the selected category of music is that night (e.g. #LoveSongsToTheLord, #KirkFranklinChallenge, #TelevisionThemeSongGospelChallenge…you get the idea!). This musician and his colleague – of course, I'm not naming names – have to roast each singer that goes live, or at least find something to make a joke about. It's all in good fun, and truth be told, it's not that difficult of a "challenge" per se, because most of these singers and musicians sound incredible. Regardless of the category selected, it's not too difficult for us as singers and musicians to find something to sing or play. It's what a lot of us have been doing since childhood, and I think it's safe to say most of us have been around church for a long time. If someone disturbed our sleep at 3:47 in the morning, I'm sure we'd roll over, stretch and scratch, reposition ourselves in bed – and begin singing from a semi-comatose state. It's not something most of us think about, to be honest – at least, it's not something I really think about.

Correction. I wish somebody would wake me from a dead sleep and ask me to sing. (Believe it or not, as much as I love to sing, there are times when I don't feel like singing.) I've learned down through the years that I am not an early-riser by nature, nor am I a morning person. And although as a worship leader, even after rising for early personal devotion, I'm still not crazy about singing at an 8am service – at least, not without a 20-ounce container of something caffeinated. You see, I'm a DAY person; daylight is my friend. I can't get enough of sunshine; I function best when the sun is out. I have a hard time in the fall and winter months when the days get shorter and sunlight is at a premium. That's my ideal time of day – when the sun is up, I find it pretty easy to sing.

On this particular day, before sitting down to write this entry, I had been singing and humming to myself pretty much all day long. It was when I was on my way home when this scripture dropped into my spirit: "Make a joyful noise unto the Lord, all ye lands." Growing up, this was a scripture that I heard quoted quite frequently. I've heard it taught in various lessons and preached from in sermons. So I had a no-nonsense attitude toward writing a devotional based on this scripture. Growing up surrounded by Pentecostal worship, I'm used to the volume being cranked up as far as the sound goes. Our worship style is not quiet – remarks were commonly made in defense of our clamorous praise, saying, "God may not be deaf, but He's not nervous either!" I could have almost written this entry without giving it much thought, but I was less than a mile from my home when I heard Holy Spirit ask me:

"How do those who were born deaf and dumb make a joyful noise?

The question brought me up short. Then He asked me another.

"How do those in underground churches in countries that oppress Christians offer Me a joyful noise?"

I'd never really thought about it. I got on my laptop when I got home and started researching. We live in America, where, currently, you can go into a Wal-Mart and begin preaching the gospel of Jesus Christ in the checkout line. (I just happened to see that video earlier in the day on Facebook.) This country has more houses of worship than you can shake a stick at; we can worship our God freely, in

Spirit and in truth. And the complaining I hear from many parishioners on any given Sunday on any given subject – from the volume of the music to the lack of air-conditioning in a building to another member not speaking to them – we've taken these liberties for granted.

However, in Somalia, there is no religious freedom; the government doesn't allow Christians to gather together publicly. There are no church buildings in Afghanistan, and even gatherings in private homes require extreme caution, the Taliban wanting to completely purge all Christians from the country. Saudi Arabian Christians risk lashing, imprisonment, torture and deportation. And in communist North Korea, 6,000 Christ-followers have been arrested and detained in the country's labor camps, and they may yet face public execution.

And yet…these are those who would rather "serve the Lord with gladness" and face death, rather than renounce their faith in Jesus Christ.

How dare we complain about trivial inconveniences and perceived slights? It's all pettiness. How dare we cop attitudes about getting up early to go to God's house and offer Him our reasonable service? I'm grateful for a voice to sing – even early in the morning, without caffeine! –

and working ears to hear the sounds of music. This country still allows me the freedom to sing my praises to the Lord at the top of my lungs — without persecution or punishment.

So what do you complain about? What keeps you from singing? And if you don't sing that well, what's keeping you from shouting to the Lord? What thing is so challenging right now that it prevents you from offering God a joyful noise? Is life so bad that you can't serve the Lord with gladness? I count it a privilege and an honor to be able to minister before Him. I'd like to think He's been pretty good to me.

Based on their devotion, there are at least 6,000 Korean Christian prisoners who think so, too...

DAILY PRAISE: Are you a timid or a bold praiser? In what way can you "live God loud"?

_____
_____
_____
_____
_____
_____
_____
_____
_____
_____
_____
_____
_____
_____
_____
_____
_____
_____
_____
_____
_____
_____
_____

God Who Sees Who I Am – and Knows My Name

The Levites who returned with them were Jeshua, Binnui, Kadmiel, Sherebiah, Judah, and Mattaniah, who with his associates was in charge of the songs of thanksgiving.
Nehemiah 12:8 (NLT)

Isn't it comforting to know that God knows who you are? This thought brings me a bit of joy and assurance to remember that the Creator of heaven and earth, as well as knowing when a sparrow falls and the number of hairs on my head, knows exactly who and where I am. In addition to that, He pays attention to what I'm doing. "The eyes of the Lord are on the righteous" (Psalm 34:15) and He knows that my service isn't in vain, as long I'm serving and working for Him with right motives and intentions. This is especially comforting to me in those times when I'm feeling insignificant and invisible – when I'm feeling like nothing I'm doing really matters. (The question "So what's the point of all of this anyway?" would fit right here.)

I can only imagine that Mattaniah was fulfilling his role in the worship of the temple, not really expecting recognition or accolades. He was a leader of an influential family amongst several leaders of influential families returning to Jerusalem at the time of the rededication ceremony of the wall that was rebuilt around the city. And he along with the other men mentioned in this verse, were all Levites. They were from families who were descended from the tribe of Levi, the tribe which was appointed by God to minister and serve before Him in His House – first in the Tabernacle, then in the Temple built by Solomon. And then, in this point in history, this specific group of Levites mentioned in this verse was going up to Jerusalem after Zerubbabel completed the rebuilding of the temple. So this group and their families were going to work in the temple, as their families had been doing for several generations. It was expected; it was the norm. It was understood by these men that after they moved off of the scene, those Levitical families who came after them would inherit the same duties and responsibilities as those which came before.

The thing is that this text makes a specific note about Mattaniah: that he and his brothers were responsible for the "songs of thanksgiving", or music for the choirs. If you do some research about Matthaniah's ancestry, you'll discover that he wasn't just a Levite; he was a descendant of Asaph. Do some more studying and you'll find out that out of 150 Psalms, 12 of them are ascribed to Asaph. Asaph was one of three men that King David assigned to be over the singing in the temple; in today's lingo, simply put, Asaph was an assistant choir director, as well as a song writer (although he may have only been a scribe to help David write his music). So Mattaniah's grandfather or great-father helped to run the Temple's Music Department before the first Temple was built. And many years later, he himself was returning to ensure that the family legacy continued.

I smile as I think of family musical legacies that continue today in this modern age. I'm certain that Mattie Moss Clark, who ran the Music Department for the Church of God in Christ (COGIC) was just rendering service that she was assigned, and all while she was raising her daughters. When she started composing music, she needed her daughters to help replicate the songs that she was hearing in her head. This took much time and disciplining of her daughters, for she wanted to impart a legacy for them of musicianship, knowing that one day the seeds she had planted would bring forth a harvest. Sure enough, all these many years later, Karen, Dorinda, Jacky and Elbernita (or Twinkie) continue that musical legacy as the internationally-known, award-winning Clark Sisters. These sisters, in turn, have passed this legacy to another generation of singers, namely Kierra and J. Drew Sheard. Of course we can't ignore that music has spread outward in the that family as well; I wouldn't dare ignore James Moss, aka J. Moss, and his contribution to this musical legacy.

I suppose that this scripture resonates with me because I've served as a choir director myself for more than 35 years. Most of that time has been spent working as the assistant to a lead director or serving under a Minister of Music. I've loved teaching, developing and leading choirs, sharing the gifts the Lord gave to me with varying numbers of congregations and audiences. There's no feeling like being able to lead a group of singers, and they in turn leading a congregation into God's presence. There were many times when, I hate to admit, I wanted to quit altogether, thinking that my contributions to the ministry were overlooked, ignored, or disregarded. There were many instances when others had no problem even taking the credit for the product of work that I and others had done. I didn't initially enter music ministry for any personal gain, but occasionally my ego was bruised for the want of just a little recognition. I don't know whether either Asaph or his descendant Mattaniah ever felt the way I did, but I certainly hope that they were better music ministers than I was, having and keeping their focus on why they were doing what it was that they were assigned to do.

Acknowledgement for my service feels good, but then Paul instructed both the Ephesian and Colossian churches that the work or service they perform shouldn't be done for recognition or because someone was watching them (Ephesians 6:6-8; Colossians 3:22-24) because God ultimately will reward us. God indeed has been kind to me, and I've had the opportunity to learn and grow and mature in ministry. If I'm serving the Lord with my whole heart, and leaving a legacy of effective service, I know what I'm doing is not in vain (I Corinthians 15:18). I must persist in doing well, because I've been promised that I will reap a harvest (Galatians 6:9). God sees me where I am, and what I'm doing. He knows my name. And pleasing the Lord is what matters above all else.

DAILY PRAISE: Have you ever felt ignored or overlooked? In those times, how has God let you know that He sees you?

_____
_____
_____
_____
_____
_____
_____
_____
_____
_____
_____
_____
_____
_____
_____
_____
_____
_____
_____
_____
_____
_____

When I'm Overwhelmed – I Will Praise

Why art thou cast down, O my soul? and why art thou disquieted within me? hope thou in God: for I shall yet praise him, who is the help of my countenance, and my God. Psalm 42:11 (KJV)

David is struggling right here. He's human. He's not discounting the word that was spoken over his life – that he was anointed and appointed by God to be the next king of Israel – and he's not forgetting what God has done for him – delivering him in the battle between himself and Goliath, and in turn delivering the nation from the imminent threat of the Philistines. But he is in a tough position right now, because he's living in exile away from home. I can imagine that he's also a bit heartbroken, because someone that he truly respected and served faithfully for years now wants to kill him. So he is forced to live away from his wife, Michal, and his best friend, Jonathan, and all of the comforts, conveniences and familiarity of home. The terrain is rough, because he's probably dealing with extremes of temperature - the dry, hot desert air, the cold nights – and probably not having enough food or drink for sustenance. He's traveling with a rag-tag, motley crew of men who have sworn allegiance to him, but being responsible for this group is not without its own headaches. He's heard

73

the grumblings of discontent from men who are probably feeling the same as David does, missing their families and wondering when David is just gonna go and take Saul's head off, so this tiresome campaign can be over and everyone can go back home. If it's not one thing, it's something else, and there's one word that can probably describe David's emotional state: OVERWHELMED.

Verses one and two say, *"As a deer pants for flowing streams, so pants my soul for you, O God. My soul thirsts for God, for the living God. When shall I come and appear before God?"*

Despite all of David's troubles, there's one thing he misses more than anything else: going up to worship in the tabernacle with the congregation of Israel and experiencing God's presence. He misses being with other believers, shouting and singing praises to their God. He longs for God's presence in this way, because right now, it seems like God is far away from him. How can God be near when He's allowed all of this calamity into his life? How can he sing when he's in a strange land, in a manner of speaking? How can he experience His presence when he's not surrounded by the sound of joyful praise and the noise of the complaints of discontented soldiers is all David can hear? He longs to return to Jerusalem, not for family, loved ones, comforts and conveniences, but to be in God's presence once again, worshipping Him.

Being away from God's presence, on top of everything else, has David feeling some kind of way. He hasn't forgotten Who God is or what He's done, but at that time, I imagine that praises weren't easily rolling off of his lips, and songs weren't bubbling over in his heart. To put it simply, more than likely, David just wasn't feeling it. However, he did look forward to the time when he could return to God's house, because he knew that eventually, God's promise in his life would be fulfilled, and the assignment that he was given would come to pass. He knew that where he was at that time was a temporary, albeit challenging, situation; David knew that the Lord would vindicate him and defeat all of his enemies. And even though he may be feeling depressed now, he could tell his soul to hope in God, because God was his salvation. The words may not have been in his mouth at that moment, but David would eventually praise God again.

There was a song I used to hear when I was growing up:

The only hope we have is in Jesus
Confusion is great in the world today
Persecution may come with such heavy weight

But we have this hope, and it's in Jesus.
— Margaret Aikens-Jenkins, composer, 1960

For me, it's not a big problem that generally bogs me down; it's usually a bunch of little things that occur in my life all at the same time. Not too long ago, I understood all too well how David was feeling, overwhelmed by circumstances and feeling pretty confused and helpless by it all. Try losing your apartment, then not having a job, having no income, then losing a vehicle all within the same short period of time. Add to that debt collectors sending you letters and calling your phone demanding payment for that which you have no resources to take care of. It may very well take the praises out of your mouth for a moment. Fortunately, although I had lost other things, I hadn't lost my memory of what God had done for me in the past. I hadn't forgotten that He was very present help in trouble. I didn't forget that He was watching over the Word that He had spoken over my life to perform it in His own time. And I remembered that He promised that He would never leave me or forsake me.

Perhaps circumstances in your life have left you overwhelmed. Maybe your head has hung down and you felt abandoned. Remember that God knows who and where you are; remember that He will ever be your Hope and your Salvation. So if you're tired, give Him a tired praise. If you're sick, give Him a sick praise. If you're depressed, give Him a depressed praise. If you're sad, give Him a sad praise. Remember, God is our Healer, our Savior and our Deliverer! In the words of Bishop Hezekiah Walker, "*Every praise — EVERY praise — is to our God!*" You may start out feeling down, but when you start to praise the Lord, you will find that He will be the Lifter of your head.

DAILY PRAISE: Have you ever felt overwhelmed by life? What scripture in God's Word, or individual came to you, or encounter have you had that helped to lift your head?

_____

_____

_____

_____

_____

_____

_____

_____

_____

_____

_____

_____

_____

_____

_____

_____

_____

_____

_____

_____

God Gave Me A Song

He put a new song in my mouth, a song of praise to our God. Many will see and fear, and put their trust in the Lord. Psalm 40:3 (ESV)

Have you ever experienced such a great deliverance that all you felt like doing is singing? You knew it was God, and nobody but God, that brought about a great deliverance in your life. Only you know how impossible the circumstance seemed in your life, how huge the mountain, how giant the…well, the giant that stood between you and your victory. God, of course, did what He said He would do, whether it was healing your body from an illness, saving an unsaved loved one, cancelling a serious debt, restoring a marriage, or providing a new car/house/job in the nick of time. Perhaps you're a brand new Christian, a babe in Christ who just received salvation yesterday, or you were someone whom the Lord delivered from a serious addiction – in either case, you knew you couldn't save yourself. Maybe you could identify with the composer of this hymn, based on Psalm 40:

My heart was distressed 'neath Jehovah's dread frown
And lo in the pit where my sins dragged me down
I cried to the Lord from the deep miry clay

Who tenderly brought me out to golden day

David must have written this psalm with gratitude, joy and a sense of relief. The Lord had defeated his enemies, brought him back again to Jerusalem and enabled him to take his assigned place as ruler of Israel. The Holy Spirit inspired him to write this for the singers in the temple; he probably couldn't wait to hear it sung, which is why he gave it to "the Chief Musician" to teach to the choir. The Holy Spirit also allowed David's pen to move prophetically, speaking of the coming of the future Messiah (vss. 7-8). This great deliverance establishes his faith in God (vs. 1), ignites his desire for others to trust in the Lord (vs. 2), prompts him to testify of God's wonderful works (vs. 10), and fuels his passion to obey the Lord in all things (vs. 4). It also underscores David's understanding of his desperate need for God as his salvation and deliverer (vss. 6-8).

The writer of the hymn continues and says it this way:

He gave me a song, 'twas a new song of praise;
By day and by night its sweet notes I will raise;
My heart's overflowing, I'm happy and free;
I'll praise my redeemer, Who has rescued me!

What song did you sing when God brought you out? Another old song that I learned at my home church was *"Tell me how did you feel when you come out the wilderness, leaning on the Lord?"* Was your heart so glad that you couldn't stop humming or singing? Do you remember a specific incident of God's deliverance that caused a specific song to spring from your heart? Or, if you have little confidence in your singing ability, did you keep a song playing on repeat (either on your iPhone or android, CD, tape cassette or vinyl – yeah, I know I'm going way back), so much so that the people around you got sick of listening to you or that recording? You know what I mean. Perhaps you didn't sing at all, but you shared your testimony with anyone within earshot. I recently heard a testimony from one of the members who sings on our worship team of what God had done for her. She turned the testimony into a real occasion, making the entire praise team dinner and bringing some good ol' soul food to our weekly rehearsal. This was on a Monday, y'all. We all rejoiced with her, praising the God who answers prayer – while eating forkfuls of fried chicken, cabbage and smoked sausage and macaroni and cheese.

God is good all the time! So are her skills in the kitchen. But I digress…

I'll tell of the pit, of its gloom and despair
I'll praise the dear Father, Who answered my prayer
I'll sing my new song, the glad story of love
Then join in the chorus with the saints above!

Believing God before deliverance happens, continually standing on His promises, stretches and exercises our faith. But something happens when we see the manifestation of His hand and He makes a way out of no way. It fixes something in our spirit. It causes us to know something, without a shadow of doubt, that we can no longer un-know. Our God, our Rock, our ever-present Help — He will deliver!

You're not singing yet? So please join me in the chorus:

He brought me out of the miry clay
He set my feet on the Rock to stay
He put a song in my soul today
A song of His praises — Hallelujah!
— "He Brought Me Out," Henry J. Zelly & Henry L. Gilmour, composers

DAILY PRAISE: Take a moment and recall when you first accepted Christ into your life. What song of praise or hymn did God give to You?

_____

_____

_____

_____

_____

_____

_____

_____

_____

_____

_____

_____

_____

_____

_____

_____

_____

_____

_____

God Is Sovereign – He's a Big God!

But who am I, and who are my people, that we could give anything to you? Everything we have has come from you, and we give you only what you first gave us! I Chronicles 29:14 (NLT)

It seems to me that we spend a great amount of time comparing ourselves to other people. We start recognizing distinctions and differences as early as childhood. The occurrence may be as innocuous as us seeing our neighbor's kid with a larger or newer toy, or our sibling eating from a larger slice of cake or a taller ice cream cone. Then the awareness may go from seeing that our hair or clothes may not look as neat or nice as someone else's, to thinking that perhaps I may not be as smart or pretty or thin as the next person. If we dwell on this for too long, this can begin to make us feel some kind of way, a bit inferior perhaps, because in general, nobody likes to feel "less than"…

Paul has instructed us about comparing ourselves to our neighbor. While there's nothing wrong about using the achievements or successes of someone else for our personal motivation, it's important to remember that we should only be working toward becoming the best version of ourselves, as God created us to be. We're all basically in the same boat; born into sin, we're all in need of a Savior, in need of redemption, and in need of reconciliation to a relationship with the Father through His Son. Now, if there's going to be any comparison made, Jesus should be our measuring stick. Because, fleshly speaking, on our best day, counting every major success and achievement we could ever reach, without Christ, we're still just sinners. Ultimately, our desire should be to be like Christ.

And how could any of us compare ourselves to Jesus Christ? How can we begin to try to compare in stature to God?

Some years ago I was watching Pastor Rod Parsley on television preach a sermon to his congregation at World Harvest Church in Columbus, Ohio. He was taking a moment to speak about God's sovereignty and God being a sovereign God. He summed it up by saying that God had defined His own sovereignty to Pastor Parsley by telling him, "I Am God – and you are not." That point may be obvious, and perhaps even a bit cliché, but, even if you don't think that statement is all that deep, it's still pretty heavy. I mean, He's God. And until I heard Him say that, the only frame of reference I had for "sovereignty" was a song that I heard Darryl Coley sing, which said, *"The Lord our God is Sovereign…He can do whatever He wants to do when He wants to how He wants to/Because He's Sovereign/God is God."*

God, to put it mildly and simply, is a big God.

I know we sing about His greatness and majesty, but have you ever pondered why in the world the Creator of the Universe - Who exalts one and debases another, Who caused things to come into existence and other things to cease to be, Who brings forth life and allows death...you get the picture – would want to have a relationship with humanity as a whole? Or, more specifically, why would He want to do something as mundane as engage in daily conversation with Him, so that He could share with me His plans, strategies and visions for my life?

That might have no impact on you whatsoever, but I find that mind-blowing.

Wilmington Chester Mass Choir recorded the song "Sovereign" and the lyrics say, in part:

Who am I to question God's wisdom? I am nothing. Who am I to question God's judgment? I am nothing.
Who am I to be offended by His way –
By what He allows to be?
– Carol Antrom, composer, 1986

David had come to the end of his life, having desired to build God a permanent dwelling place. After contributing and collecting the finest resources and turning this task over to his son, Solomon, David offers a prayer of praise to the God of Abraham, Isaac and Jacob, recognizing everything that He is and everything that He has. David acknowledges the task at hand and invites God to search his own heart, to know that his motives and intentions are pure and filled with integrity. He prays for his son's heart that it may desire to seek and obey the Lord's commandments, and he prays for the nation of Israel that they may always desire to obey God. But in the middle of this prayer, David recognizes that for all that he was offering, every resource, all the materials to build the temple, had come from God Himself. There was no comparison of what he could do to what God could do; there is no comparison between who we are and Who God is. David was a great king, but he knew that he himself would be nothing at all without the King of all Kings on his side.

I heard someone once refer to God as "the Great Big Little Bitty God". He's great enough to create and occupy the entire universe, but He's small enough to live inside of me. Oxymoronic, yes. But I'm glad it is so.

DAILY PRAISE: What has God given to you that you can give back to Him?

_____

_____

_____

_____

_____

_____

_____

_____

_____

_____

_____

_____

_____

_____

_____

_____

_____

_____

_____

_____

_____

_____

_____

_____

_____

_____

_____

_____

_____

_____

_____

_____

_____

_____

_____

_____

_____

_____

_____

_____

_____

_____

_____

_____

_____

_____

_____

_____

Celebrating With The Song of My Life

Rise up, O LORD, in all your power. With music and singing we celebrate your mighty acts. Psalm 21:13 NLT

"I wrote a song about it. Like to hear it? Here it go!" – "Calhoun Tubbs", portrayed by comedian David Alan Grier on the sketch comedy series "In Living Color"

I love a celebration. I gravitate toward anything that feels like a party. It doesn't really matter to me whether the celebration takes the form of a church service, a concert, a wedding, a baby shower, a backyard barbecue, or meeting friends for a birthday dinner at a restaurant – with someone bringing cupcakes for the celebratory dessert. Most of these occasions have a few things in common: a gathering of people, of course; food (although some venues don't allow food or beverages in the main part of the performance venue); and music – even restaurants have some sort of background Muzak playing in the background.

As part of the culmination to a 3-week standup comedy seminar, I was given the opportunity to perform a set at a comedy night with real, professional and more experienced comedians. Writing jokes was a bit challenging but all I really needed to do was put a spin on stories from my real life. Of course, I talked about being a Christian woman, but I wasn't just any kind of Christian. I was Pentecostal. So I had to provide a description to those in the audience who weren't as familiar with my denomination. What I wound up saying was, "Think about the best party you've ever went to, the last concert you attended, and the last sporting event you went to. Take all of that energy and activity, put it together, shove it in a church for two to three hours, and that is a Pentecostal service on a Sunday morning!"

(This was a secular event, not a Christian one, and the audience was primarily filled with nonbelievers. So it felt good when that joke got a big laugh. But I digress…)

If anyone ever had a reason to celebrate, especially for what God had done for them, it was David. God Himself called David a "man after my own heart" (Acts 13:22), and the Lord granted him favor and greatly blessed him. He was anointed king over Israel, empowered to slay Goliath, protected while being pursued by Saul, eventually vindicated to return home and take his place as king. God also was on David's side so that he and his men could defeat the Philistine army.

God later granted David mercy to return the Ark of the Covenant back to Jerusalem, first from the Philistines, then from the house of Obed-Edom. That last occurrence provoked David to such a praise that he danced out of his clothing (II Samuel 6:13, 14; I Chronicles). The priests carried the ark; the Levites played all of the instruments, comprising the orchestra; the singers made up the choir; David danced before the Lord with all of his might, and all of Israel praised the Lord their God with mighty shouts of joy. Now that sounds like a party on the move.

So what did David do? He wrote a psalm about it. Like to hear it? Here it go...

Well, I won't print it here, but what appears in I Chronicles 16:8-36 is the psalm that he wrote and gave to Asaph and his brothers to learn and sing before the Ark of the Covenant. Parts of this psalm also appear in Psalms 96 and 105. And what David wrote...well, the remarkable thing is that David wasn't only writing about events from stories told to him down through the years. He wasn't only writing what he had learned about the God of Abraham, Isaac and Jacob. He was telling story in song - his own testimony. He was writing from first-hand experience about what God had done for him. And since David was a prolific songwriter, he wrote about what the Lord had done for him over and over again. He wrote about God's majesty and might, His goodness, faithfulness and mercy from whatever circumstance he was dealing with — whether he was running through the deserts, or sitting on the throne, whether he was filled with indignation at his enemies, or David himself was broken and repentant. The songs he composed and sang to the Lord were based in his own life story, and they are now a part of the permanent record of the wonderful works of God. More than half of the Psalms were composed by the blessed and grateful king.

So what does your song sound like? Even if you don't sing, let me suggest that your story can become a song, however long or short, however contrived or simple. The Lord wants to hear you sing to Him your song about what He's done for you. Maybe you haven't killed giants or routed armies, but there is nothing too mundane about your own life for which God can't receive the praise, glory and honor. Did He save you? Has He provided for you? Has He made ways and opened doors? Has He healed you? Then rejoice! Praise! Dance! Sing to Him! Celebrate our great God! Give God praise with the song of your life!

DAILY PRAISE: The Lord wants to hear you sing your song to Him about what He's done for you. What does your song sound like?

_____

_____

_____

_____

_____

_____

_____

_____

_____

_____

_____

_____

_____

_____

_____

_____

_____

_____

_____

_____

_____

_____

_____

_____

_____

_____

_____

_____

_____

_____

_____

_____

_____

_____

_____

_____

_____

_____

_____

_____

_____

_____

_____

_____

_____

_____

The Sacrifice of Praise That Honors God

Whoso offereth praise glorifieth me: and to him that ordereth his conversation aright I will shew the salvation of God. Psalm 50:23 KJV

The sacrifice that honors me is a thankful heart. Obey me, and I, your God, will show my power to save. Psalm 50:23 CEV

I was having a discussion not too long ago with some church members in a class setting about some of the sacrifices and offerings required back in the Old Testament times. It was an agrarian, or agricultural, society, where growing grain and raising livestock was common, so the resources for Old Testament offerings were readily available, if your family owned the property and the means to do so. Since most of the offerings or sacrifices asked for were from bulls, goats or sheep – or pigeons or turtledoves, if the family was poor – it's safe to say that everything involving this ritual – from raising and cultivating the animals, to transporting them, to the actual killing of the animal or bird – was rather messy business. Everyone in the class couldn't rightly imagine this entire production of these kinds of offerings, but we were all very glad that we didn't have to fool with any of that now and that our offerings

97

involved bringing other things — like cash or debit cards.

From the times when sacrifices were offered on a stone altar, they fell into different categories. These offerings are introduced in the first five chapters of Leviticus.

1) <u>The Sin Offering</u>: mandatory atonement for and confession of and forgiveness of sin — a bull, a goat, a pigeon or fine flour needed to be offered
2) <u>The Trespass Offering</u>: mandatory atonement for sin and cleansing from defilement — a ram
3) <u>The Burnt Offering</u>: an act of worship which expressed devotion, commitment and complete surrender to God — a bull, ram or bird
4) <u>The Grain Offering</u>: an act of worship that recognized God's goodness and provision — comprised in part of grain, fine flour, olive oil and baked bread
5) <u>The Peace Offering</u>: an act of worship representing thanksgiving and fellowship, establishing communion between God, the priest and the worshiper — any unblemished animal would do

These offerings were offered by the priests every day, sometimes twice a day, with the quantities sometimes varying based on whether it was the Sabbath, holy days, or one of the Feast Days. As you can see, God required a worshiper to bring some kind of offering, whenever they came to worship. Imagine always having to bring something from your herd or from your flock, or carrying with you the currency of the day to purchase that which was to be sacrificed. And these offerings were a temporary covering for sin, not a permanent solution. This sounds like a real production.

I'm grateful for Jesus becoming our Ultimate Sacrifice so that we would no longer need someone to stand between us and God; we don't need a High Priest to act as a mediator for us. Since the Veil was ripped in two, each of us can now go boldly before the Throne of Grace "to obtain mercy and grace to help in time of need" (Hebrews 4:16). Jesus' blood satisfied God's justice and answered the sin problem which kept us from a personal relationship with God.

Hallelujah! No more bulls, goats, sheep or birds that we have to bring whenever we go to worship. That doesn't mean however we come before the Lord empty-handed. We still present offerings to our God, albeit in a slightly different form.

1) <u>A broken spirit and a contrite heart</u> (Psalm 51:16, 17). A worshiper that comes in humility is everything to God; pride has no place in praise.

2) <u>Prayer</u> (Ezra 6:10). Prayer is like sweet-smelling incense wafting up to God's nostrils. He loves communion with us

3) <u>Thanksgiving and Praise</u> (Psalm 100:4; Hebrews 13:15). He wants that we continue to sing psalms, hymns and spiritual songs, making melody in our hearts to him (Ephesians 5:19).

4) <u>Joy</u> (Psalm 27:6), expressly for the reason of deliverance from our enemies.

5) <u>Hospitality and generosity</u> (Hebrews 13: 16), especially to those in need. These are the sacrifices that please God.

6) <u>The tithe</u> (Malachi 3:10), because there is both a promise and a curse attached to it, depending on our actions. It's the one place in scripture where we can actually test God and see what He'll do.

7) Perhaps the best offering that we can give to God is <u>our obedience</u> (I Peter 2:5, 8, 9) as well as our diligence to be

a witness for Christ. Our obedience to God's Word surpasses any other act of worship we perform. God would have that, because it's the best offering we can give him (I Samuel 15:22).

If we want to really see God's salvation, we must do all we can to align ourselves with His Word. That's not to say, though, that we don't need to sing praises if we are obedient, or that we don't need to give tithes and offerings if our hearts are broken and contrite. Jesus reprimanded the scribes and Pharisees for being so careful to measure out amounts of spices and herbs, but neglected matters of the law, being loving, faithful and merciful to others (Matthew 23:23). We should be mindful to offer all of those gifts to the Lord. Our total obedience to His Word allows His glory to be revealed in our lives and His power to be demonstrated in the earth.

DAILY PRAISE: Since you don't need to bring livestock or fowl to the House of God as an offering, what sacrifice do you need to offer more to the Lord?

_____
_____
_____
_____
_____
_____
_____
_____
_____
_____
_____
_____
_____
_____
_____
_____
_____
_____

Praise God, My Teacher

My troubles turned out all for the best – the forced me to learn from your textbook. Psalm 119:71 The Message

As I write this entry, I am staring at a bunch of middle school students at a school that I'm not really familiar with. This is a very interesting situation. The vast majority are working on their given assignment, some others are sitting quietly, working on other things, and yet some others are doing all they can to avoid causing a disturbance in the room, even though it may require a bit of effort on their part. However, I'm certain that the vast majority of them would rather be somewhere else other than the classroom they presently sit in. It may be that, like I did when I was a kid, they are thinking to themselves, "What do I need to know this stuff for anyway? I know I'll never use it."

(To be honest, I never thought that about English class, which I loved. This sentiment leaned toward courses like Finite Math, History and Chemistry – all classes that I thought were a colossal waste of time.)

Allow me to clarify a few things. At the time of this writing, I work as a Substitute Teacher for the Jefferson County Public School System. I've been delegated the authority by the school system to administer the lessons of a full-time teacher who happens to be absent from their classroom on any given day. The teacher leaves lesson plans (or ideally, they do), and I facilitate the teaching on their behalf for that day, endeavoring to create a productive environment in which the students can learn and complete assignments. To be more specific, I'm what you call a Preferred Substitute Teacher, which means that I work primarily at one school every day. On days that the school has no assignments for me, I can choose an assignment at another school within the system. But most of the time, I'm at a particular high school, which shall remain nameless. It is a high school, and since I've spent a lot of time there over the last couple of years, I've been able to develop many relationships with the people there. I've communicated with a lot of the teachers that I've subbed for, and have developed a good relationship with the principal, vice principals and administrative staff. All of the security detail got to know my name pretty quickly since the first day I worked there, greeting me every morning I showed up.

But most of the relationships I've developed are with the students, having spent one or several days in a single classroom with them. They've gotten to know me, and I've gotten to know them. Some of the kids hate to see me coming – I'm pretty strict when enforcing classroom expectations – while other students think I'm pretty cool, calling me "the best sub" or their "favorite sub" in place of other teachers. While I'm not at the school to be liked, or to be anybody's friend, it does feel good to have gained a bit of respect from even the most troubled of students. Wouldn't you know it, they've expressed similar sentiments about some of the courses they have to take, like Social Studies, Algebra 2 and History of Visual and Performing Arts. If I had a dollar for every time a student has complained to me, "Ms. C.! I don't see why Geometry is so important anyway! It's not like I'm ever gonna use it after I graduate…" or "What I need to know History for? I don't give a -------- about World War 1!" I am quick to tell my kids at the high school that taking these courses instills more into them than just facts and information. It gives them a repository of knowledge to pull from when they need to replicate it in a paper, or a quiz, or an end-of-semester exam. The students can also learn things like critical thinking and time-management, while also developing discipline, determination and persistence.

(Another group of middle schoolers has entered the room since I started writing this entry…)

The author of Psalm 119, seemingly unlike a lot of my students, placed great value on God's Word and learning God's statutes. He may not have understood it in the beginning, but he discovered that everything he was experiencing and learning was working for his good. I can imagine that, similar to high school freshmen assigned a research paper or taking a quiz, test or major exam, the beginning of hard life experiences made the author ask, "What's the point of all this?" But over time, he could internalize what he was learning so that he could draw from it later on if he needed it. Psalm 119 speaks repeatedly of the author's appreciation for God's laws, statutes, commandments, precepts, and principles that were better than life to him. God's Word provided illumination ("…a lamp unto my feet…"), sure footing ("…order my steps in your Word…"), peace to those who loved it ("…and nothing shall offend them") and was satisfying to those who obeyed it ("…sweeter than honey from the honeycomb").

It's safe to say that a productive high school senior can look back at the end of their high school career − at all they needed to learn and produce to succeed − and say that for all of their challenges they are indeed better, smarter, more disciplined, more accomplished than they were when they started. So are those who strive to study, learn and apply God's Word to their everyday lives. It will indeed be the thing we can stand on when facing challenges of our own, and if we allow it to shape us, we are all the better for it. The graduating senior has a diploma to look forward to; the believer who trusts the unchanging, infallible promises of God can anticipate an eternal reward.

(Some kid has decided that he wants to act up. I'm about to tell him that he needs to try Jesus…don't try me…)

DAILY PRAISE: Every affliction is for our spiritual growth. What lesson do you thank God for learning, even though it seemed painful at the time?

_____

_____

_____

_____

_____

_____

_____

_____

_____

_____

_____

_____

_____

_____

_____

_____

_____

_____

_____

_____

_____

Praise is My Weapon – Well, At Least One of Them...

I praise you, Lord! You are my mighty rock, and you teach me how to fight my battles. Psalm 144:1 (CEV)

I've never been a good fighter. It seemed that when I was a kid, that's all anyone that I knew wanted to do – get into a fight and beat somebody up. Even now, I'd rather shy away from a conflict; I think that if we can talk it out rationally, without strong emotions or yelling or screaming, then why not solve the problem that way, instead of figuratively or literally coming to blows? I wasn't the kid who ran to a fight, or even looked for one. I was that kid who ran fast and far away from what might be coming.

Thinking about it now, I know I must have been an easy target. I was skinny and wore glasses; I was bookish and as my mom would say, I "lived in my own world". Although I desperately wanted to fit in and to be liked, I was rather socially awkward, rather wanting to read a book or watch TV than to play outside with kids my age. See, my mother had married into a very large family who was very urban and street savvy, while I was rather naïve and, well, a real nerd. I was gullible, willing to believe what anybody told me, and that often put me at the mercy at my stepfather's family, especially those who were to become my cousins. Yeah, I was easy prey. I talked rather "proper" for a child under the age of 10 years old, and I didn't really know how to relate to them. So, when one of my new relatives decided to toughen me up and teach me "how to fight", I didn't know really what to do — or how to escape the situation. More often than not I ended up with bruises and scratches on my body as a result of these "lessons", and my cousins just couldn't understand what my tears were about.

Now, you must understand, I came up in a culture where defending yourself was a matter of pride, not only for oneself, but for your family. It was very common practice that if you got in a fight and lost, when your parents found out, you'd get whipped and punished for losing the fight! Well, anyway, that is what happened to me...

I recall one time when I was with my stepfather's youngest sister walking through the neighborhood and some girl started yelling at us, talking real smack. My aunt tells me to yell something back at the girl, and like a dummy, I did it. This exchange went on for a few minutes, with the girl cussing at me and me parroting backtalk via my aunt. Finally, the girl threatens to come up the street to where we were and beat me up. Echoing my aunt's suggested verbiage, I recall saying, "Well, come on, then!" Much to my surprise, the girl got to where I was lickety-split, and even more to my surprise, my aunt, who had goaded me into this position, stepped back away from the altercation and proceeded to watch as this girl whipped my tail. I mean, she used me to clean the concrete. Interestingly enough, though, when my aunt recounted this tale to my parents and the rest of the family, she reversed the roles, making me the victor and the other girl the loser. My family cheered for me — they were never so proud as to hear that I had won a fight.

I definitely was not like David. He was a man of war, a skilled fighter and soldier. He was a military man, but he wasn't trained to fight in King Saul's army. He demonstrated his prowess before both the army of Israel and the Philistine army when he took out Goliath. But even that wasn't his beginning; David had cared for his father's flocks in the wilderness, protecting the animals from being slaughtered by lions and bears (oh, my!), and killing both predators. David gives praise to God for always being right there with him and teaching him how to fight and win battles. I'm sure that he probably knew how to use every weapon at his disposal — probably the bow and arrow, sword and slingshot were the most common — but he gives credit to the Lord God of his fathers for training him in what he needed to know. He grew from being a single fighting man into a military strategist over Israel's armies, expert in the art of war.

Now the New Testament lets us know that challenges will come to knock us down and take us out, but that the weapons that we use to fight our enemies are not carnal, but are mighty through God (2 Corinthians 10:4). He's given us both weapons and armor that we as believers need to always appropriate for ourselves (Ephesians 6:11) so that we can effectively fight. We must remember that the purpose of the armor of God is not necessarily for us to run to chase down and attack our enemies, but so that when we are attacked, we can stand in the evil day. And once we do all we know to do – praying without ceasing, studying His Word, holding fast to His promises, praising God that He will do just what He said, believing that the weapons may form but they won't prosper – we simply use that armor to continue to stand. It's not us who are fighting, per se, but it is God who fights for us. It's the Lord Who promised that He would never leave us or forsake us. He won't allow our enemies to defeat us, even if we take a hit and get knocked down – and He won't leave us alone to be embarrassed by our foes.

He trains us by allowing life to happen to us in order to drive us to Him on our knees to pray, and to His Word for instruction and revelation. I know that as long as God is for me, He is more than the world against me. I know that in every situation, He has already caused me to triumph and has made me more than a conqueror through Him Who loved me.

DAILY PRAISE: Praise is one of the weapons that we use. With the weapons that we use for spiritual warfare, how have you learned to fight?

_____

_____

_____

_____

_____

_____

_____

_____

_____

_____

_____

_____

_____

_____

_____

_____

_____

_____

_____

Wow, God! That's Extraordinary!

Oh that men would praise the Lord for His goodness, and his wonderful works to the children of men! Psalm 107:31 KJV

It's Monday. I suppose it could be any day of the week, but the weekend was long and I'm tired. Mondays are just Mondays, when sometimes you have to make yourself get back into the grind of the work week and making a living. You may not be looking for any change in routine, or expecting anything out of the ordinary. There's nothing wrong with that, but it's always a great thing to occasionally experience serendipity, or something particularly and surprisingly pleasant. Good. Wondrous. Even extraordinary. It's good to see or hear or experience something you know was really mind-blowing, in a positive way.

That happened to me on this day. Perhaps nothing significant to anyone else, but it immediately inspired this entry in the devotional.

The morning began normally. It wasn't unusual for me to not have an assignment at my regular school and to take another assignment at that institution of learning. I arrived there, got the classroom information and directions and headed off. The students were spending this period in another classroom per se, so I went to this room to find the instructor and get any rosters or sub plans he may have for the absent teacher. This other classroom was located in a vocational section of the building, where trades such as HVAC, carpentry and welding were taught. Well, at this particular moment, the instructor whom I was retrieving my class from taught masonry. In other words, he was an expert in building structures with bricks, mortar and the like. Before I returned to my assigned classroom, he wanted to show me something that he and the students had built over the course of the semester. We walked into the construction area and he showed me something built with brick and mortar and the like. However, it was when he walked over to the structure and switched it on that my day got a little more interesting.

Initially the structure he showed me was just bricks and mortar, with an opening on the back of it and some rocks in the base of it. From looking at it, I judged it was about the standing height and length of my Nissan Sentra. But the instructor walked to one side of it and either plugged it in or flipped a switch, then walked to the other side and turned on a gas tank of some sort. Then he turned on the blow torch he was holding and ignited the rocks in the base. The structure simultaneously began to run water and burn fire. A waterfall fire pit – who would have thought it? I had never seen anything like it, but I could imagine something like that sitting on a patio in someone's back yard; because it was so nice, and so well-constructed, I could see it being photographed and showcased in anything from a masonry catalog to an upscale home in a home design magazine. Quality!

And then the instructor once again told me that he had showed the students how to build it. The thing this instructor kept telling me was, "It wasn't that hard to build." Sure, I'm sure it wasn't for him, the experienced builder. I'm sure the students didn't start out feeling that way. The class was presented that idea of the structure without a prior blueprint being shown to them; all they had to do was to trust and follow the instructions of their teacher. The product that came forth was, in my opinion, a job well-done. They built a structure (I don't know another word to use – forgive me the redundancy) that both was a waterfall and a fire pit. I find that rather amazing. Remarkable. Yes, even extraordinary.

The psalmist recounts in Psalm 107 how God had demonstrated His love for His people Israel, more specifically those who were in a bad way and really needed His help. The psalm draws different scenarios of difficulty that his people experienced. In verses 6, 13, 19 and 28, those who found themselves in whatever bad situation they were in had enough presence of mind to call upon the Lord in their trouble. They understood that, for all of their abilities and blessings, they could not get themselves out of their own messes; they couldn't deliver themselves. But God was merciful to His people, and He brought them out of their distresses. This was reason and cause for His people to praise their God, as repeated in verses 8, 15, 21 and 31. While it was a challenge for the people in the situation and unable to see their way out, I know that it wasn't anything too hard for God. Their troubles didn't take God by surprise, and with every deliverance, with every victory won, His people could learn to trust Him more.

Oh, and the word *"wonderful"* that the writer continues to use in the Hebrew means "extraordinary". Man's abilities are limited – even with all of our resources and skills. But I used to hear a pastor say frequently when I was growing up that "man's extremity is God's opportunity." Whenever God makes a way for us when there seemed to be no way, we have a right, a reason and a responsibility to praise Him.

Jesus, Jesus – how I trust Him!
How I've proved Him o'er and o'er!
Jesus, Jesus, precious Jesus –
Oh, for grace to trust Him more!

— "'Tis So Sweet to Trust In Jesus," William J. Kirkpatrick and Louisa M. R. Stead, 1882

DAILY PRAISE: When was the last time God did something so amazing for you it blew your mind? Who needs to hear that testimony from you?

_____
_____
_____
_____
_____
_____
_____
_____
_____
_____
_____
_____
_____
_____
_____
_____
_____
_____
_____

Give God a "Yet" Praise

Though the fig tree shall not blossom, nor fruit be on the vines, the produce of the olive fail and the fields yield no food, the flock be cut off from the fold and there be no herd in the stalls, yet I will rejoice in the Lord; I will take joy in the God of my salvation. God, the Lord, is my strength; he makes my feet like the deer's; he makes me to tread on my high places. To the choirmaster: with stringed instruments.
Habakkuk 3:17-19 ESV

We don't know that much about Habakkuk, other than that he was a prophet whom God spoke to. It appears that he may have been a Levite, someone who regularly served in the temple, and possibly someone who had some connection to the music department, because of the musical directions that come up in chapter 3. During this discourse with the Lord, when the Lord is pronouncing judgment upon Judah, Habakkuk received such powerful messages wrapped in beautiful imagery, such as what we still refer to today:

Write the vision, and make it plain upon tables, that he may run that readeth it. (2:2)

For the vision is yet for an appointed time, but at the end it shall speak, and not lie: though it tarry, wait for it…. (2:3)

…But the just shall live by his faith. (2:4)

But the Lord is in his holy temple: let all the earth keep silence before him. (2:20)

All of these things are uttered while the Lord is revealing to the prophet about the impending doom and calamity that will befall Judah. The Lord tells Habakkuk that He will use the Chaldeans (aka the Babylonians) to chastise His chosen people for their disobedience, and to bring them back in line. However, He reassures Habakkuk that He will also punish the Chaldeans for their oppression of Judea. And while this conversation is going on, Habakkuk does what we so often do, but we've been directed so many times not to do: in short, he questions God's wisdom. In other words, Habakkuk's attitude was like, "God, don't you see what's going on? Don't you hear me praying to You? Do you know what You're doing?"

It's a wonder to me that Habakkuk was permitted to stay alive long enough to get the message and — well, write the vision...

How many times have we experienced our own devastation and calamity and cried out to God, but it seemed as if our prayers went no further than the ceiling? I know I've had my own discourses with God about losing my job, losing my car, being evicted from my apartment, etc. My lament didn't stop with my own troubles, however; I had no problem questioning God about the pervading illnesses and death of loved ones in other families, the poor state of certain neighborhoods, the violence in our communities, the growing state of apathy toward the less fortunate by our politicians and those who are in government…I could go on and on. And I've cried out to the Lord, and know of others who have as well; we could feel our collective frustration rising as we waited for something to happen, for a change to occur…as we waited for God to show up.

The turning point comes when we remember Who it is that we serve, and that He has never come short of His word. The old folks used to say that "He's a doctor that's never lost a patient, and He's a lawyer that's never lost a case!" It's at this time of trouble that we remember – that is, if we have a working memory – what our God has done for us before, and since He's a God who never changes, that same God will do it again. Habakkuk puts that in his prayer (which turns out to be a song, since the passage in chapter 3 is written to be accompanied by music) when He prays in 3:2, "…*Revive thy work in the midst of the years*…" In other words, Habakkuk says, "Lord, I've heard about what You did before. Do it again!"

Our responsibility, then, as was given to Habakkuk as well as to the nation, was – and is – to wait.

Nobody likes waiting. I don't like waiting; I don't consider myself to be a very patient person. But you can be sure that I won't be sitting idle in the meantime. And neither would Habakkuk, for as long as he would keep serving in the temple. His resolve was, as ours should be, that even in the face of challenge, trial and tribulation, he would remember Who God was, what He had done in the past, and what He promised to perform in the future. The vision would speak and not lie; the Lord is in His holy temple, in control of everything; the just would live by his faith in the promises of God. The Lord would do it again.

Habakkuk also took upon himself an additional responsibility: to rejoice in the Lord His God, even in the face of calamity. He wasn't choosing to praise merely because he knew that God would eventually deliver them out of the hands of the Babylonians, no. He praised God for the strength that would sustain himself and His people through the season of difficulty. God would be their source of courage, make their feet steady and sure (like a deer walking over rocky terrain) and make them to walk with certain confidence despite the mountain of difficulty. I imagine that he rushed to give this to the temple orchestra once he had written it down. I don't know for certain, but with this prayer set to music, Habakkuk may have been hoping that every time this song was played, it would be a reminder to the people – or whoever was listening – of Who God was, what He had done, and what He would yet do, as well as the strength He would be for them while they waited. So…will you trust Him while you wait? Will you choose to rejoice?

DAILY PRAISE: What do you trust God to do for you? What challenges do you choose to rejoice in the face of? Who else can you encourage to rejoice today?

_____

_____

_____

_____

_____

_____

_____

_____

_____

_____

_____

_____

_____

_____

_____

_____

_____

_____

_____

_____

_____

I Can't Tell It All – But I Can't Wait To Tell It!

They shall eagerly utter the memory of Your abundant goodness and will shout joyfully of Your righteousness. Psalm 145:7 (NASB)

I suppose it's safe to say that David was, among other things, a skillful songwriter and musician. This particular psalm is the only one in the Book of Psalms that's named "A Psalm of Praise of David", which is another way of saying that it was specifically a *tehillah*, or a hymn. It's filled with such exaltation and boasting about the greatness of David's God; I can imagine him, as he was writing, being filled with so much gratitude that he could burst! Or, perhaps, just burst into song! Have you ever felt so excited about something that God has done for you that you just couldn't contain it? You know, you would start talking about the goodness of God and before you know it, time has flown by, the sun has changed positions in the sky, errands that were scheduled have been postponed, and your audience has either one of two responses: a) they're trying to be polite, but they start thinking of excuses to get away from you, or b) they're now so engaged in the conversation that they start testifying themselves. At least, these are responses that I've encountered...

I recall one instance during the years when I was traveling on public transportation, back before I purchased my first vehicle. Let me take a moment and give kudos to the Transit Authority of the River City, or TARC, whose buses and system of routes were, at one time, one of the best in the region. For many years I traveled to church, school and back home again on the bus; if I had any other destination in mind, believe me – TARC would take me there. Church members used to joke that because of the way I traveled around the city of Louisville on TARC, I had accumulated more miles on me than a lot of their cars! Of course, time on buses means time to meet and talk to people – this was during a time before smartphones and social media! These days, if you want to engage anyone, you have to friend or follow them on SnapChat, Instagram, Facebook or Twitter, and you're more likely to see a fellow bus rider with their head down in their phone...

I also got to know a lot of bus drivers. I started riding the bus with an adult when I was 6 years old; I began riding solo at the age of seven. Bus drivers got to recognize me over time since I was a daily passenger; they would even go so far to wait a minute or two when I was transferring from another bus, because they came to expect me and any other regular riders. Travelling to the same place for many years — first to schools, then eventually to a job — allowed me a lot of time for conversation and getting to know my friendly, neighborhood bus driver — and there were many. As I was saying (a couple of paragraphs ago — yeah, I know, I know), I was talking to one of the drivers one day, and we were conversing about life and some of the challenges that I was dealing with at that time. I guess my situation was just a matter of fact, but my description of the situation (and I have no recollection of what trial I shared with him) sounded so overwhelming, it prompted him to ask, "So what is your stabilizing agent?" Or, in other words, "How in the world do you keep from losing your mind?"

What did he ask that for? Immediately with no hesitation I replied, "The Holy Ghost!" I proceeded to share about the goodness of God and His grace in my life, and how He kept me from taking drugs and alcohol in order to deal with my crap. I told him that were it not for the grace of God I probably would have killed myself. I shared with him probably a dozen different ways that God had showed up in my life, how He had shown Himself faithful and that I simply had to trust His Word while I waited on Him. I talked so much and so long that by the time I was near my destination, he finally just remarked, "I didn't ask for all that."

Perhaps the driver wasn't expecting "three points and a poem", so his response was less than enthusiastic, especially because he was a captive audience. It's just that when God has shown Himself mighty to you, if you have a working memory, and a sense of gratitude for what He's done, it's difficult to keep your story to yourself. Praise is not about how we feel at any given moment; it's about how well our memory works. If we remember not just what He's done, but Who He's shown Himself to be, then we will be overflowing with stories ready to share. The things we go through are not just for ourselves, but to create in us an encouraging witness for someone else who needs to know that God is a deliverer! He is mighty to save! He will supply every need! He's merciful and compassionate and hears every prayer! And He's the only One Who can satisfy the longing in our hungry soul! Who wouldn't serve a God like this?

What's that old song? *"I said I wasn't gonna tell nobody, but I couldn't keep it to myself, what the Lord has done for me!"* And why would you want to keep your story to yourself? Go and tell somebody! At the very least you can quote the words of another old song:

When I think of the goodness of Jesus
And all that He's done for me,
My soul cries out, "Hallelujah!" —
Thank God for saving me!
— Composer Unknown

DAILY PRAISE: What was it that God did for you that made you want to run out and tell everyone what He had done? What was it that you couldn't keep to yourself? Who do you feel would benefit from your praise report?

_____

_____

_____

_____

_____

_____

_____

_____

_____

_____

_____

_____

_____

_____

_____

_____

_____

_____

_____

Praise in the Face of Fear

Do not be afraid or discouraged, for the Lord will personally go ahead of you. He will be with you; he will neither fail you nor abandon you. Deuteronomy 31:8 (NLT)

I know that we as believers aren't supposed to admit to ever being afraid or anxious, but it's probably a more common state of being than not. It's safe to say for as long as we're above ground, there are going to be some situations where we are going to feel alone, perhaps even out of our depth, maybe like we're even drowning. That overwhelming feeling can sometimes leave us speechless; in an extreme situation, it's absolutely paralyzing. Fear can be a monster. But we can't share that with anyone – we don't want to say the words, "I'm scared." Isn't that an admission of a lack of faith?

I guess that's why the Bible contains several scriptures which contain the command "Fear not." It's said that this statement, in one form or another, appears 365 times in scripture – that's one exhortation for every day of the year (except for the extra day in a Leap Year, like this year, 2016, for instance). The Lord knows that there are things that we will face in our lives that will appear scary, whether it's facing a bully, completing an assignment, starting a business, dealing with the diagnosis of a disease, or stepping into a new phase of life, like with marriage or beginning a family. God promised us from the outset that we don't have to face life's situations by ourselves — He promised not to leave our side.

I recall a very scary situation that I didn't believe I was ready for. I received an opportunity to lead a group of singers for a tour in another country; because I was excited about the offer, of course I said yes. I traveled to another city here in the states in order to receive the training about everything I needed to know to lead this team. The days ticked by, and still I waited to get this information about how to successfully lead this tour. I suppose it was due to circumstances beyond our control, but I never got the information, never had the sit-down with the powers-that-be for the training. Suddenly, it was the day of departure, and fear had already crept in, telling me that I would fail. And I was terrified. But I had to move forward and get on that plane, with only the reassurances that I would do a wonderful job leading the team.

I had no idea what awaited me when I got off of that plane. From day one and for the next 31 days, everything that could go wrong did go wrong. And horribly. It was Murphy's Law on steroids. The touring vehicles broke down, not once, but twice. The tour manager from that country, young and brand-spanking new, had issues with handling the money. Winter storms made travelling very difficult. Two tour members took very ill while we were supposed to be performing concerts just about every night. Once, I locked the keys to everyone's room in an already empty building…don't ask! And I had my own issues spending money and keeping records of receipts and accounting. In addition to all of that, I had difficulty regularly reaching and speaking to the person who owned this company and ultimately was in charge of everything, because they were in another country outside of the USA as well, and therefore in a completely different time zone. Here I was twenty years older than almost all of the people on this team, and they were looking to me for leadership and answers, all the while being thrown into one embarrassing situation after another.

I'd like to say I made all of the right decisions and handled every difficulty with grace and wisdom. The awful truth was I had no idea what I was doing, and furthermore I had no business leading this tour. I was first scared out of my mind at the prospect of this assignment, then I wanted to walk out in front of a truck – I made mistake after mistake. I wanted to dig a hole and bury myself in it. Mercifully, but embarrassingly, leadership was given to someone else, so I spent the rest of the tour as an Indian, not a chief. I later realized that as much I had been praying, complaining and crying to God, I learned a lot of in the midst of that challenge. I also realized that He had answered my prayer: I didn't want to be tour manager, and God answered that request.

When Joshua received the baton of leadership from Moses, he was given the responsibility to lead the Israelites across the Jordan River. God promised that He would destroy the inhabited nations and the people would take possession of the land. There would be battles to fight and challenges to deal with. What a "monster" of a task ahead of him! I'm not sure whether Joshua faced this new challenge with calm confidence, or if he was scared out of his mind. Either way, Moses encouraged Joshua by saying that the Lord wouldn't abandon them or fail them, so he and the people didn't have to be afraid or be discouraged. In light of God being on their side, they had every reason to "be strong and be courageous." Moses repeats that same charge – once to the people of Israel, and once directly to Joshua.

I don't know if there are any scary situations you're facing right now, but He promises us repeatedly in His word that we don't have to be afraid. We can be strong and of good courage. As a matter of fact, not only are we promised His presence, He promises us His peace. Paul instructs us to not *"worry about anything; instead, pray about everything. Tell God what you need, and thank Him for all he has done. Then you will experience God's peace, which exceeds anything we can understand. His peace will guard your hearts and minds as you live in Christ Jesus."* (Philippians 4:6, 7 NLT)

We don't have to fear. We must trust God that He will take care of our monsters!

DAILY PRAISE: When was the last time you took God's Word in order to "stand and be courageous"? What scary situation did you experience God's peace in?

_____

_____

_____

_____

_____

_____

_____

_____

_____

_____

_____

_____

_____

_____

_____

_____

_____

_____

God Thinks About Me! Go Figure!

How precious also are thy thoughts unto me, O God! how
great is the sum of them! Psalm 139:17 KJV

I am a thought in the mind of God
A single iota in the imagination of the Almighty
I am that which preceded the words which called to
my substance
I am God's daydream before my consciousness was
formed
And who am I, that He should think of me at all?
  - "Love Object", by myself

He has me on His mind. Crazy, isn't it? To think that
the Creator of all that we know, and some many
things that we don't, thinks about me. Or, to put it
more accurately, He thought about me. See, I
started as a thought in the mind of God. The
Omniscient, Only Wise God put thought into my
creation and existence.

The single thought, which is me, was filled with
God's purpose for my life. Just imagine: God's idea
of me is filled with potential – everything I'm
supposed to be and everything I'm supposed to do
filled that thought. Once again, I guess I have to
amend my own thoughts, because I realize that
since God is Ever-Present, He lives in the eternal
Now, so it's probably more accurate to say that all
of God's intention that is named Tiffiany Nicole

Collier fills <u>that</u> thought (present tense). My gifts, talents, acquired skills and abilities, my personality and my proclivities, all of my character traits, and all of the stuff about myself that I've not yet discovered or become aware of — all of that is in God's idea of who I ultimately am.

You think that's something? His thoughts about me are so major and significant, He wrote a book about me. His idea of me filled a single book. And because God is Who God is, and He doesn't do anything in a small and insignificant way, I imagine that my book is a best-seller. It's the story of His plan, purpose and destiny for my life. I'm not just making this up, either. Psalm 139:16 says, *"Your eyes saw my unformed substance; in your book were written, every one of them, the days that were formed for me, when as yet there were none of them* (ESV)." I believe that that book contains every blessing He's supposed to pour out on my life, every plan that I'm supposed to walk out, and every life that will be impacted by my existence on this earth. I also imagine that He wrote this book around the same time He was conceiving Jesus' death on Calvary and the redemption of mankind; Revelation 13:8 kind of gave me that idea.

It really doesn't matter what kind of day I'm having either — I might think I have it together sometimes, but other times I may not be doing so great. I know me. I've experienced a few years where it seemed that I was doing pretty well, but more often than not, I went through several years when I felt like I couldn't do anything right. I thought that the world had conspired to constantly knock and keep me down, that I was a complete failure and totally worthless. That's the way I thought most of the time. However, after reading God's Word, I'm reminded that God doesn't think of me that way. Psalm 139:14 says, *"I will praise you, for I am fearfully and wonderfully made; marvelous are your works, and that my soul knows very well* (NKJV)." God thinks I'm a marvelous work. I wrote about this in my poem, which says in part:

Who am I to argue? He would know –
The very crook of the fingers of His right hand testify
As he reaches into the earth –
He lifts a scoop of dirt up toward His waiting lips
And then, never waiting to exhale, He blows –
Blows into this clay His Living Breath

He made me, so of course, He knows all about me – everything: the good, bad and ugly. He knows my successes and achievements as well as my screw-ups and my hang-ups. He knows how I think. He knows what makes me tick – and He knows what ticks me off. He's knows me better than I know me;

He knows my deepest heart's desire, but He also knows that my heart is *"deceitful above all things and desperately wicked"* (Jeremiah 17:9). But I do know that the thoughts He thinks about me are to bless me and not to harm me – to give me a future and a hope (Jeremiah 29:11). So I must be careful not to "follow my heart", because I can't always trust it. I can, however, put my trust in God, because at the end of the day, I know He loves me with an everlasting love, and that He'll never leave or forsake me. So whenever I'm feeling particularly fat, having a bad-hair day or not doing so well while facing a life challenge, I choose to align my thoughts about me with His thoughts about me.

Let me stop having this be all about me, and let you know that He's written a book about you, too, that began with a purpose-filled thought. His story for you may be different than the story He's written for me, but His thoughts toward you are the same – He's wild about you! I mean He's madly, passionately, over-the-moon gone over you! And His thoughts are filled with all the good things in store for us if we only continue to trust Him. So…what's in your book?

DAILY PRAISE: God's written a book about you that contains His plan, purpose and destiny for your life. What's in your book?

_____

_____

_____

_____

_____

_____

_____

_____

_____

_____

_____

_____

_____

_____

_____

_____

_____

_____

_____

_____

_____

_____

Praise to God, My Security (Better Than ADT!)

But let all who take refuge in you rejoice: let them ever sing for joy, and spread your protection over them, that those who love your name may exult in you. For you bless the righteous, O Lord; you cover him with favor as with a shield. Psalm 5:11, 12 (ESV)

There's an expression that I use from time to time, sometimes to encourage other people, but a lot of times I use it to encourage myself: "Faith comes by hearing. Faith operates by speaking. And praise is the language of faith."

The Word of God bears witness to this as it pertains to faith coming by hearing (Romans 10:17) and faith operating by speaking (Mark 11:22, 23). But David gives faith-filled believers who trust the Lord a reason here in Psalm 5 to, as many would use the common cliché, "praise God on credit." And this is not to say that a believer should only praise God in expectation of deliverance; we should give God praise because He is good. I don't believe it's possible to write an encyclopedia of reasons as to why we should praise God; John the apostle probably summed it up best by saying *"the world itself could not contain the books that would be written* (John 21:25)." However, the Book of Psalms offers at least 150 different reasons why the Lord is worthy of our praise. Or, at least that many reasons.

David himself contributed to half of those reasons. The good king not only recounts what God has done for him; at every turn, he (as well the other contributors to the Psalms) repeatedly encourage believers to give God praise for as many of those reasons. We are encouraged to praise individually and with others, from our beds and in the sanctuary, whether we're in the valley or on the mountaintop. We're directed to praise whether we're experiencing the heights of joy or the depths of despair. Our present condition doesn't matter. Our state of mind is irrelevant. Even our spiritual condition, positive or negative, doesn't disqualify anyone from declaring the goodness of God. Our praise isn't dependent upon how good we've been; it's all about how good God is. To be clear, that doesn't mean we can live ratchet lives and expect our every praise to be acceptable to Him. I'm only saying that if we truly understand that He is a good God, we should want to bless Him with our whole being.

Feels like I went off on a tangent there, doesn't it?

God is a protector and a deliverer. David knew it. Many individuals in biblical antiquity could and did testify that God was a shelter, a shield, a fortress. His name is a strong tower (Psalm 18:10) where we can find safety; Psalm 46:1 says that He is our refuge and strength, a very present help in trouble. Psalm 91 recounts all the kinds of protection that God provides when we put our trust in Him and he describes all of the benefits to those who hold onto Him in love.

I'm not for sure how well 10-year-old Willie Myrick knew his Bible, or how strong his relationship was with the Lord. But in the spring of 2014, God showed this child that He was indeed a deliverer. Here this boy was minding his own business in the front yard of his house, when some guy comes along and snatches him up, puts him in his car and drives away. I don't know how scared this kid was, or what his kidnapper was planning to do with him. I don't even know if the child knew the scripture where God says, "*When he calls to me I will answer him. I will be with him in trouble. I will rescue him and honor him*" (Psalm 91:15). The news outlets didn't share all of that information.

What we do know now is that Willie knew a song, a song made popular by Bishop Hezekiah Walker, which says "Every praise is to our God/Every word of worship with one accord/Every praise, every praise is to our God." We know that he sang that song for the three hours he rode around in the kidnapper's car. So, we also know that Willie's personal fear didn't stop his praise. Any thoughts toward the unknown outcome didn't stop his praise. The cursing and threats from his abductor didn't stop his praise. And we can probably conclude that by the time Willie's captor released him, he had probably learned the words to that song, too – words that will follow him until he gives his life to the Lord.

God indeed spread his protection over Willie Myrick, and covered him with His favor. Willie knew to sing praise to the One who would be his safety and his deliverer. Willie is learning at a young age how to speak this "language of faith." If praise is indeed the language of faith, it would serve us all well to increase our praise "vocabulary" and to learn how to speak this "language" fluently.

DAILY PRAISE: How have you experienced God's "favor like a shield" over your life? For what specifically can you rejoice when God has been your refuge?

_____

_____

_____

_____

_____

_____

_____

_____

_____

_____

_____

_____

_____

_____

_____

_____

_____

_____

_____

_____

_____

_____

Choose to Be Thankful

In every thing give thanks: for this is the will of God in Christ Jesus concerning you. I Thessalonians 5:18 (KJV)

He is here – God is here
To heal the hopeless heart and bless the broken.
– "God is Here," Martha Munizzi

The sacrifice of thanksgiving is mentioned several times in the Old Testament. It was the one type of offering that was completely voluntary; it was offered by a worshipper who wanted to express gratitude for God's goodness. The sacrifice of thanksgiving, which consisted of cereal, oil or bread, was offered along with the peace offering, which could be any unblemished animal. This sacrifice was offered willingly, motivated by a heart filled with joy.

This offering was also an act of communion between the worshipper, the priest and God. Other sacrifices, such as the sin offering or the trespass offering, were either totally burnt on the altar as an offering to God, or they were partly burnt on the altar and partly eaten by the priest. However, as a piece offering, after the Lord and the priest received their portions, the worshipper could return home with whatever bread/grain and meat was left over, to prepare a feast with for their family and friends. There at this feast they would celebrate the peace with God, a relationship with Him and the blessings that flowed from Him.

Thanksgiving is indeed a choice. But it should be a choice that we make daily, in light of God's goodness and mercy toward us. Thanksgiving isn't just a matter of giving thanks, or merely saying "thank you" for some beneficial act toward us. It goes deeper. I looked up the word "thanksgiving" in this verse, and ran across a familiar term: *eucharistos* (yoo-KHAR-is-tos). It's a transliteration, the short definition being "thankful, grateful", but it's really made up from two words meaning "well" and "grant freely". Like I said, it goes deeper:

> "…properly, *thankful* for God's grace working out what is (eternally) *good*; grateful, which literally means "*grace*-ful" (*thankful*) for God's *grace* (what brings His eternal favor)." — from HELPS™ Word Studies

I had seen the word "eucharist" before. It's not a word that's commonly used in my religious circles, but I remembered that some denominations use that word to describe the sacrament of communion. Of course I had to look it up again, but as you can see, it's proper definition makes no reference to the New Testament communion as we know it. And then I discovered in Wikipedia that the verb form of "eucharistos" was used by the Apostle Paul when describing Jesus and the Lord's Supper:

*For I have received of the Lord that which also I delivered unto you, That the Lord Jesus the same night in which he was betrayed took bread: And when he had **given thanks, he brake it,** and said, Take, eat: this is my body, which is broken for you: this do in remembrance of me.* I Corinthians 11:23, 24 (KJV, emphasis mine)

Several things from these scriptures about thanksgiving jumped out at me:

1. I find it interesting that Jesus would bless - or give thanks for - something as menial as bread, and then turn around and break it. Then again, the animal's body had to be broken for the peace offering, in conjunction with the sacrifice of thanksgiving. That bread in Jesus' hands represented his own body, which would be offered up for us, for our peace with God, so that we would no longer be strangers, or

foreigners, or enemies of God. And this, of course, was after the Father had blessed and approved His Son before the world.

2. As believers, we've been blessed by the Father, and yet, we experience brokenness in our own lives, whether through trial or self-abasement, because the Lord won't despise a broken spirit or a contrite heart (Psalm 51:16, 17). It's in these situations when we are encouraged to look at God's grace toward us, despite challenging circumstances. Paul tells us to give thanks in every situation — it's God's will for those of us who are in Christ Jesus, because He is working everything out for the good (Romans 8:28) to those who love Him and who are the called according to His purpose. This is why I frequently say, "If I can't thank God *for* it, I will thank Him *in* it!"

3. Giving of thanks and breaking of bread seem to go together, particularly for groups of people who gather together, as they did in the early

church (Acts 2:46, 47), fellowshipping with one another and celebrating God's favor and His goodness toward them all. Christ's physical body was broken for us, that we may have peace with God; now, we are all members of the Body of Christ on earth, carrying with us the gospel of peace to those who are still away from Him. That peace should motivate us in all that we do as a Body, especially in our conduct and treatment toward one another – and for this, once again, we are instructed to be thankful (Colossians 3:15).

In light of all that God has done, let us choose to be thankful. In everything.

DAILY PRAISE: Write down those things that you know you're thankful for. Then answer this question: what situation do you choose to be thankful *in*?

_____

_____

_____

_____

_____

_____

_____

_____

_____

_____

_____

_____

_____

_____

_____

_____

_____

_____

_____

_____

Our Hearts Will Sing...

Speaking to yourselves in psalms, hymns and spiritual songs, singing and making melody in your hearts to the Lord; Ephesians 5:19 KJV

I'm a musical mutt. I appreciate all types of music. If someone were to ask me what kind of music or what style of music I like, I would more than likely reply, "If it's music, I like it!" I have a personal preference about what I listen to regularly, or what I purchase, but I believe that every style of music has its place in our world.

Back in the 70s when I was a kid, I was exposed to a variety of music. In our home, when my mom was married, my stepfather had a catalogue of R&B and Soul albums that he added to regularly. These vinyl recordings, which contained the music of then up and coming artists, are considered vintage and classic now. I would frequently wander down to the basement where the stereo system was and peruse the album covers of artists like Al Green, Marvin Gaye, Isaac Hayes, the Jackson Five, Earth Wind & Fire and Stevie Wonder. I also recall seeing the faces of female artists as well: Aretha Franklin, Gladys Knight & the Pips, Dionne Warwick, LaBelle, and Diana Ross and the Supremes. These artists received airplay on the only R&B radio station in the city, and this radio station, 1350AM WLOU, eventually went off the air every night at midnight.

Well, I spent my summers with my stepfather's family at his mother's house, and when I would sleep over on the second floor with my step-aunt, she would leave the radio on all night long, and we would listen to a pop/Top 40 radio station that played music 24 hours a day, so I would hear artists like Barry Manilow, Barbra Streisand, Neil Diamond, Elton John and Olivia Newton-John. And during the school year, attending a mostly-white private school, I was exposed to what my classmates listened to, which was classic Rock music: KISS, the Doobie Brothers, Fleetwood Mac, Pink Floyd and David Bowie. Some of my classmates were deep into Country & Western, and with them I listened politely to Dolly Parton, Loretta Lynn, Willie Nelson, George Jones and Johnny Cash. However private school also introduced me to the more serious classical music sounds of Beethoven, Mozart, Bach, Handel and Brahms, and I was even taken on field trips to see the ballet, opera and orchestra performances. My musical palette was being developed at a young age.

That didn't change when our family became Christians, though my mom and stepfather were separated by that time. The first gospel album that I ever saw in our house was by Walter Hawkins and the Love Center Choir. So the music that I listened to was still multicultural – we listened to both Traditional Gospel and Contemporary Christian radio stations. In our home, you would just as often hear the Imperials as you would hear the Mighty Clouds of Joy, both Shirley Caesar and Sandi Patti, the Winans as well as Petra, the Clark Sisters as well as Amy Grant.

All styles of music have their place. It can all serve a purpose if used correctly. Music was created by God to reflect, reveal and minister to what's going on in the human soul. Paul told the church at Ephesus that our daily walk should reveal the power of God through our relationship with Jesus Christ. Trials may come but we don't need to act the way the world acts; we don't need to indulge in carnal behavior, and we don't need to yield to every fleshly desire and craving. Our walk should be purposeful and intentional, despite challenges, and instead of satisfying ourselves with wine or other spirits, we need to be filled with the Holy Spirit. We should allow the Holy Spirit to provoke us to encourage ourselves and each other, using:

Psalms: specifically one of the writings from the book of Psalms, accompanied by sophisticated instrumentation — an orchestra or band. This was the most common music used in Old Testament temple worship.

Hymns: well-known songs which gave praise to Jesus Christ, the God-man. These became the songs that were sung in the New Testament church. Modern-day hymns are said to hold sound Biblical theology and can be an aid to instruction.

Spiritual Songs: songs that are sung under the inspiration of the Holy Ghost. They may be a prior composition but are mostly spontaneous in nature, ministering both to God Himself and other people, when offering testimony of God's goodness and power, as it exhorts to other believers.

Each type of music here is to be used to encourage and edify one another, as well as to provoke oneself to give thanks, or to maintain an attitude of gratitude. These styles of music are all employed in the modern worship experience today, with only the particular genre of music varying, depending on the culture and the congregation that sings it. Its primary purpose, as Paul relayed it to the Ephesian church, is to encourage gratitude in the hearer and the singer, and to maintain gratefulness at all times. It matters not whether your psalm, hymn or spiritual song is sung as a classical anthem, a reggae piece, an Irish folk jig, a bluegrass tune or a rock ballad — so long as it always gives thanks to God, in the name of our Lord Jesus Christ. Keep singing. Keep praising. Whatever you do, don't let the music stop.

DAILY PRAISE: Use this space below to pen your own song, hymn or spiritual song that you can use to encourage and uplift someone else.

_____
_____
_____
_____
_____
_____
_____
_____
_____
_____
_____
_____
_____
_____
_____
_____
_____
_____
_____
_____
_____

God Gives Me A Reason To Laugh

He will yet fill your mouth with laughter, and your lips with shouting. Job 8:21 ESV

I love to laugh. I can be very solemn most of the time, probably I have a lot on my mind. At least that's what my mother and some other folks have said over the years. Believe it or not, I like to laugh; it's just that some things that make other people laugh I don't necessarily find funny. I don't watch most sitcoms on TV, and I don't go to the movies to watch most comedies – especially if they star folk like Ben Stiller, Will Farrell, Adam Sandler or Steve Carrell. Slapstick comedy or toilet humor is lost on me. I could be in the midst of a group of people who are laughing at something they saw, or something they heard, or even just a story that's been told – and half of the time, I'm clueless as to what the joke was. I don't even bother asking anymore what is so funny; people just kind of shrug as if to say, "You just missed it." I guess I have a different sense of humor.

Which is interesting these days, because it seems that I've been able to make a lot of people laugh. I can be sharing a story from my life with some friends or colleagues of mine, and they will just burst into laughter. And a lot of the time, it's not the subject matter that's particularly amusing; it may just be the way I'm telling the story. I had the opportunity to perform a stand-up routine in a club setting with some other professional comics who do it for a living. It's not something I'm trying to make a living at; it just so happened to be the culmination of a three-week comedy workshop I took part in order to add something to my acting arsenal. I learned that performing comedy is partly about timing – it's the way you tell a story about something that actually happened in real life. You take an actual situation and if you can make people see the absurd in the situation, chances are you can make them laugh. There are other techniques that you can use to enhance your storytelling, and I learned in the workshop that the right cocktail of story, timing and techniques can tickle someone's funny bone.

The following is part of a story that I actually shared at this comedy night; this really did happen to me, and it illustrates the absurdity of a situation quite well. I'm a single woman who has been attending church conferences since I was a kid. There are thousands of people who attend these conventions, many of whom are single brothers – eligible, marriageable, heterosexual men. None of whom, for some reason, have looked in my direction for any other reason than friendship.

Well, a few years back, I was at one of these conferences, and this woman stops me and asks me for a safety pin to fix a broken closure on a skirt she wanted to put on. This was a relatively conservative crowd, and she didn't want to walk into a church service with her jeans on. She had on a nice wig, and her makeup was flawless; the only thing she wanted to change was her jeans. "I don't want to embarrass my pastor," she said. Unfortunately, I didn't have a safety pin to give her. I wished her well, and went on my way. I couple of hours later, I ran into this woman again at my hotel; she was wearing the skirt. I remarked at her fortune and we struck up a conversation. In the middle of our talk, she leans over to me and says, "I'M A MAN." This person leans back, we finish talking and we go our separate ways. The absurd thing is that I'm a single woman at this conference, and with all of these eligible, marriageable, heterosexual men, the one man that decides to talk to me is wearing a skirt!

(This got a giant laugh from the audience, by the way...)

I'm so glad to know that God laughs, too. God felt first every emotion that we as humans feel; remember that we are created in His image and after His likeness, so it makes sense that He built us with emotions. The Bible speaks of God being angry, and jealous, and loving, and compassionate. God is a spirit, so built into the fruit of the Spirit is joy. God sees the absurdity of mankind's efforts to fight God – and to plot against His people, His righteous ones (Psalm 2:4, 37:13) – and He laughs! God loves humanity, and desires to save us from ourselves, even when we curse Him and desire to have nothing to do with Him (that is, humanity as a whole, not followers of Christ). And how does He react? What is His response? He laughs. He actually has a sense of humor about the matter. He knows that His enemies don't stand a chance; He knows that those weapons that may form against His people will never prosper.

We can laugh even in the midst of adverse circumstances if we remember that the Lord is on our side! Laughter is good for our whole being, mind, body and spirit; it's like good medicine (Proverbs 17:22), and His joy, or rejoicing in the Lord, is our strength (Nehemiah 8:10). Joy is a part of rejoicing, and joy isn't the same as happiness, which is based on "happenings", or life's external conditions. However, joy is an internal work of the Holy Spirit; it's a force of the power of God that can fuel our confidence in the promises of God – Who He is and what He's done. Think about your favorite athletic team (the particular sport doesn't matter) and how you cheer them on whenever they play a game. This is what the Lord does for us: He causes us to shout and cheer at the fact that we are on the winning side! He brings laughter to our souls so that we can meet every challenge with excitement and hope. Are we as believers in Christ Jesus powerless? Are we afraid of what man can do to us? Do we shrink at the trials of life that come? That's absurd! We are more than conquerors through Him Who loves us! He shelters us in the time of storm, and we can stand tall with our heads above our enemies; this is why we can sing and rejoice in the God of our salvation. The joy of the Lord can cause me to laugh in my trouble. No matter what, in the end, I win. Now, that's funny.

DAILY PRAISE: Sometimes life just doesn't make sense. What was the last absurd thing you encountered – and how did God make you laugh at it?

_____

_____

_____

_____

_____

_____

_____

_____

_____

_____

_____

_____

_____

_____

_____

_____

_____

_____

_____

Praise God, Who Answers Prayer

I will sing to the Lord, because He has dealt bountifully with me. Psalm 13:6 NASB

Hallelujah! He's an Answering God!
Hallelujah! He's an Answering God!
I prayed in Jesus' Name and by faith the answer came –
Hallelujah! Hallelujah! He's an Answering God!
– Composer Unknown

Earlier in the day that I wrote this entry, I was in the studio with my producer working on my music. I've accumulated quite a few songs that I've written, and it'll probably take a minute for them to all be recorded. But I don't write songs for the express purpose that they may be recorded; I write in order to express what's in my heart at the given moment. Some of my songs tell stories, some encourage people to keep the faith or exhort them to praise God for His goodness. A good number of the songs I write are prayers to God – they address Him in a very specific way, whether I'm celebrating for what God has brought me through, or I'm petitioning for help when I'm struggling with something. I guess you could say that they all are prayers in one form or another, whether I'm praying for myself or for someone else.

My Christian experience started with me being surrounded by music and song. I spent a good amount of time either listening to the radio or records or cassette tapes, or at church listening to other people sing. These were people whose voices sounded so good in my ear I never thought I could hear anyone better, and that included the folk that I heard on the radio. I learned a great deal from these adults as I listened to their testimonies or sat under them as they preached and taught from the Word of God. I was 12 years old when I gave my life to Christ, and it wasn't too long after that that I began to realize that Christianity wasn't just about the good singing or great music I heard. I was about a real relationship with God through Jesus Christ, and that meant that for me to build a relationship, I needed to talk to God. Every day.

My prayers as a kid, of course, were rather self-centered. "God, would you please bless me with XYZ?" or "Lord, could you bless our family with the money to go out of town to the Council/the Convention?" I was just learning to pray, but it was something that our mom did with us every night. Oh, yes – my mother made me pray out loud every other night, although there were three of us in the house, she, my sister and I. Now that I think about it, I don't remember hearing my sister pray aloud in our circle…anyway, I learned what words to say by listening to my mother pray. Now, she was a single mom who did her best to raise us. We didn't have very much growing up, although there were members of our church who were very kind to my mom and our family, but over time I became painfully aware of how little we had. I learned to pray so that our family's needs would be met, and I would watch as God would make a way for us over and over again. He didn't always give us what I thought we should have, but He always blessed us with what we needed.

As I went first through college and then out on my own, I encountered my own struggles in life, whether with needs that had to be met, or with relationships, or tasks that needed to be completed. Over the years I learned that the more I prayed, the more I needed to pray not just for needs, but just to spend time with God. I learned that not only could I tell Him anything, but if I waited and listened, He would speak to me, too. It would be real two-way communication. Sometimes He would say Yes, other times No, sometimes Wait. But the most frustrating times were the times that I would be in the middle of a real life challenge, and I would be met with silence from God! Those were times when I really needed the Lord to speak, but I would hear nothing. An evangelist once shared this thought: "The teacher is always silent during a test." And while I was trying to figure it out, in the words of a songwriter, God had already worked it out!

David is lamenting in this Psalm about the hard times he experienced and how he felt like God had forgotten him. But somewhere in this Psalm David acknowledges that God answers prayer; he knows this because of God's track record in his own life. David chooses to trust and rely upon the Lord, because he can remember all of the other prayers that he's prayed and all of the other petitions he's sent up — and even though the answer may not have come how David wanted it to, God did answer. David then sings about God's goodness. What's all this about prayer, you ask? Well, the word "bountifully" in the Hebrew (*gamal* or gaw-MAL) means "to deal fully or adequately with"; think of a pregnancy that comes to term, or a fruit or vegetable that is cultivated to the peak of its ripeness and is ready to be picked. It connotes that our good God has overseen our situations to bring about His expected end, and in the end, His answer is for the Highest Good. Sometimes the answer is great rescue and deliverance; other times His answer involves the allowance of loss or pain. While we may not understand the answer we receive or the outcome He allows, everything is working together for the good, all in accordance with His purposes. He knows the plans that He has for us: plans to bless us and not to harm us — plans for a future and a hope.

He is a good, good God. God hears and answers prayer. In the words of Travis Green, He's intentional — never failing. So I'll sing: "I don't have to worry 'cause it's working for me!"

DAILY PRAISE: Think of something significant that you've prayed about recently. What prayer has the Lord answered for you in the last month?

_____

_____

_____

_____

_____

_____

_____

_____

_____

_____

_____

_____

_____

_____

_____

_____

_____

_____

_____

_____

_____

_____

_____

Praise God With a Childlike Heart

And they said to Him, "Do You hear what these children are saying?" And Jesus replied to them, "Yes; have you never read [in the scripture], 'OUT OF THE MOUTHS OF INFANTS AND NURSING BABIES YOU HAVE PREPARED AND PROVIDED PRAISE FOR YOURSELF'?" Matthew 21:16 Amplified

Since working as a substitute teacher, I have done all I can to avoid taking an assignment at an elementary school. Here at the end of the school year, assignments get scarce, so the assignment pickings are slim. I need every working day to go onto my last paycheck, I had no choice but to take this particular assignment, on the day before the last day of school. The day starts later at an elementary school, but it's a longer school day. I arrived at an unfamiliar place, got my room assignment and details from the secretary in the Main Office and took what seemed like the long walk down to the classroom. I walk into the room and memories flooded back to my days as a primary student, with the pictures on the walls, graphics and images in primary colors on the tables and carpeting, numbers and the letters of the alphabet all around me, labeled cubbies where children could stow their backpacks and belongings. This kindergarten teacher — yes, you heard me right, kindergarten — worked with an assistant. This teacher's assistant was present (thank God!); she had been given the plans and was very familiar with the daily routine for the students.

I observed, and endured, all of the situations that fueled my reluctance to take the job in a primary setting in the first place, but by the end of the school day, I have to say, it wasn't as bad as I'd thought. An elementary school setting has a specific structure which works for the benefit of both teachers and students. You have to have a certain disposition and level of patience in order to regularly deal with little people – little people who constantly want your attention and need your help with one thing or another. Little people have a lot of energy and require that you be on your feet for most of the time. Little people are very trusting, and while they may try to push your boundaries, they'll ultimately follow your directions because they very much want your approval. After I left the school, I began to think on that experience with these kids and how their existence paralleled so much with what a walk with Christ should look like:

1. These kids who had never seen me before immediately trusted me. One after another would walk up to me every few minutes and either tell me

something about another student ("Ms. Collier, he took my crayon!"), let me know they weren't feeling well ("My ear hurts when I swallow."), or to inform me as to how things worked in the classroom ("We each have our own crayon boxes!"). They allowed me to touch their heads and faces to check out their ailments, and let me take their hands to lead them in walking down the hallway to the lunchroom. While they were assembling their Memory Booklets and going around the room to get other students to sign their books, they asked for me to put my autograph in their books, too.

2. They felt safe in the classroom because I was always there to watch them. These students can't stay still for very long; they're constantly wriggling and squirming and popping up out of their seats, so I had to keep my eye on them to make sure that no one in the room did anything that could potentially hurt another student – like running around the room with a sharpened pencil, kicking another

student who sat near them or lifting up a chair in the air to move it. I either intervened or gave directions in several situations because I saw what could potentially happen.

3. They followed the directions I gave them even if they didn't want to, and I had to repeat myself several times until they got the gist of what I wanted them to do. It made for a more peaceful and productive atmosphere and these little people had the freedom to complete their tasks with little disruptions.

Ah, the exuberance of youth! I was fortunate to come to Christ as a child, and the lessons and stories I learned as a child stay with me until this day. It's written in the Gospels that Jesus said that it's with a childlike temperament and attitude that anyone can come into the Kingdom of God. A child's heart is more honest and their motives are more pure. The sound of their earnest voices isn't something that can be ignored. Jesus quoted from Psalm 8:2 about how God had prepared and provided a source of praise for Himself – a source comprised of the purest of hearts and most honest of motivations. This pure, honest praise would silence God's enemies. How pure and how honest is your praise? How much do you trust that He's watching you, that He has His eye constantly on you? How badly do you want God's attention and how earnestly do you want to seek His approval by doing what He says?

DAILY PRAISE: Do you have children? In what way can they teach you about trusting and pleasing God?

_____

_____

_____

_____

_____

_____

_____

_____

_____

_____

_____

_____

_____

_____

_____

_____

_____

_____

_____

_____

_____

_____

Praise God. Period. (You're Breathing, Ain't You?)

Let everything that hath breath praise the Lord. Praise ye the Lord! Psalm 150:6 (KJV)

Let everything that has breath and every breath of life praise the Lord! Praise the Lord! (Hallelujah!) Psalm 150:6 (Amplified)

The Hebrew term for praise in this passage is *halal* (pronounced haw-LAL), that is defined, in part, as "to shine, hence, to make a show, to boast, and thus to be (clamorously) foolish; to rave, causatively, to celebrate..." The charge that Psalm 150 gives to us is not a directive to be quiet, by any means. We are to be more than just audible and visible; our boasting needs to be demonstrative, and our demonstration needs to be loud! We're supposed to make a big deal about the God that we serve. Do you know what qualifies you to praise the Lord, to boast about the Lord, to speak well of Him, to lift up His name? Here's how you know: inhale. Exhale. If you can inhale and exhale, you are qualified to praise. The dead can't praise Him, so if you're above ground, that charge is for you.

The last phrase in that verse, "*Praise the Lord!*" in Hebrew is actually a compound word using the words *halal* (praise) and *Yahh* (the Lord). So "Praise the Lord!" in Hebrew is actually translated to English as the word "Hallelujah!" As a matter of fact, the verse can actually be read as, "Let everything that hath breath, Hallelujah! Hallelujah!"

In Psalm 148, the command is for kings, princes and judges; it's for young men and young women; it's for the elderly and for children. However, praise isn't only for mankind. The charge to praise is given to the celestial beings, the angel armies, sea monsters, lightning and hail, snow and fog, stormy wind, mountains and hills, fruitful trees and all cedars, beasts and all cattle, creeping things and winged birds.

Scripture clearly shows us when we should praise God: we are to praise at all times. In sadness and in joy. In plenty and in want. In victory and in defeat. When we feel like it and when we don't. Scripture instructs us why we praise God: for Who He is and for what He does. We thank Him because He is good. We praise Him for His wonderful works. We bless Him for all of His benefits. We worship Him because He is holy. We sing to Him because He created us. We enter His gates with thanksgiving and we enter His courts with praise – because He is good!

It's a statement of purpose. It's a reason for existence. It's inclusive in its scope and intentional in its meaning. It's a cry, a charge, a command and a cause. It's a right, a reason and responsibility. It's permission, a privilege and a qualifier. Praise is where He is enthroned, it's His place of habitation – praise is where God loves to hang out.

Praise is both a time and a place – it's both where, and when, God sits down. It's both the appointment and the meeting place where God *receives*. He is The Audience of One Who receives our attention, our ministry and our entertainment. He receives our exaltation, our magnification and our glorification of Him. He receives our gratitude, our blessing, our honoring and our worship toward Him. And He receives all of our offerings of praise – not because He needs to receive it, but because we need to offer it. And when He sits down, His intention is to spend time with His beloved. Praise is our entrance into intimacy with the Almighty.

Moses and the children of Israel did it. (Moses wrote a song about it. Like to hear it?) Joshua led Israel to do it before the walls of Jericho came down. Gideon led an army of 300 to do it before a battle. Deborah did it after defeating a Canaanite king – she wrote a song about it, too. David did it as a shepherd, as a musician, as a warrior, as a fugitive, then as a king. The prophet Elisha called for a minstrel to do it in the presence of King Jehoshaphat. Angels did it in the presence of shepherds. Elizabeth did it in the presence of the baby Jesus in Mary's womb. Mary did it, too – and she wrote a song about it. The crowds did it for Jesus in the streets. Children did it for Jesus in the temple. Peter and the apostles did it after they were beaten. Paul and Silas did it in prison – and made the jailhouse rock!

Inhale. Exhale. The mere fact that my lungs expand and contract allows me the opportunity to praise the Lord. Praise isn't predicated on my feelings; I need only a memory of what He's done. Praise isn't based on how good I've been – it's all about how good He's been. And I don't need a choir, a praise team, musicians or instruments to accompany my praise. I don't need to be in a church at all to praise. I've been in my living room, my kitchen, my bathroom, my bedroom; the front seat of my car, walking down the street, standing in the park, laying on the grass under the stars. I don't know what I'd do if I couldn't praise the Lord! I don't know everything about praise and I'm still learning, but I do know that there is power in praise! His presence is in every place where my praise is. I can do it by myself, but I'd rather praise the Lord with you! *Oh, magnify the Lord with me, and let us exalt His name together!*

Lift Him up! Lift Him up
'Til He speaks from eternity;
He said, If I, if I be lifted up from the earth
I'll draw all men unto me!
— "Lift Him Up," Johnson Oatman Jr. and Benjamin B. Beall, 1903

DAILY PRAISE: What is today's reason for giving God praise? Who else do you want to include in your "praise party"?

_____
_____
_____
_____
_____
_____
_____
_____
_____
_____
_____
_____
_____
_____
_____
_____
_____
_____
_____
_____
_____

About the Author

Tiffiany N. Collier has been involved in music ministry – including songwriting, musical arrangement and leading worship – for over 35 years. Growing up at Greater Bethel Temple Apostolic Church in Louisville, Kentucky, she served as a choir director from the age of thirteen, for both youth and adult choirs. Tiffiany worked not only in the local church, but also as Minister of Music and Assistant Minister of Music on both state and national levels. She's traveled and performed with several gospel musical stage productions. She recorded and toured in the states with Min. Tommy L. Jones and the Christian Mass Workshop Choir as well as touring internationally with the Glory Gospel Singers, under the leadership of the group's founder Phyliss McKoy-Joubert. She conducts music seminars and workshops covering various subjects including vocal technique, praise and worship leadership and choir decorum, and also provides vocal coaching to individuals and groups. She currently serves as Worship Leader for Kingdom

Worship Praise & Worship team of Kingdom Fellowship Christian Life Center, under the leadership of Pastor Timothy E. Findley Jr.

Made in the USA
Middletown, DE
27 April 2022

64844366R00116